not limited to But

(SMATTERING 2)

by tENTATIVELY, a cONVENIENCE

Through the eye of a needle

in a haystack press

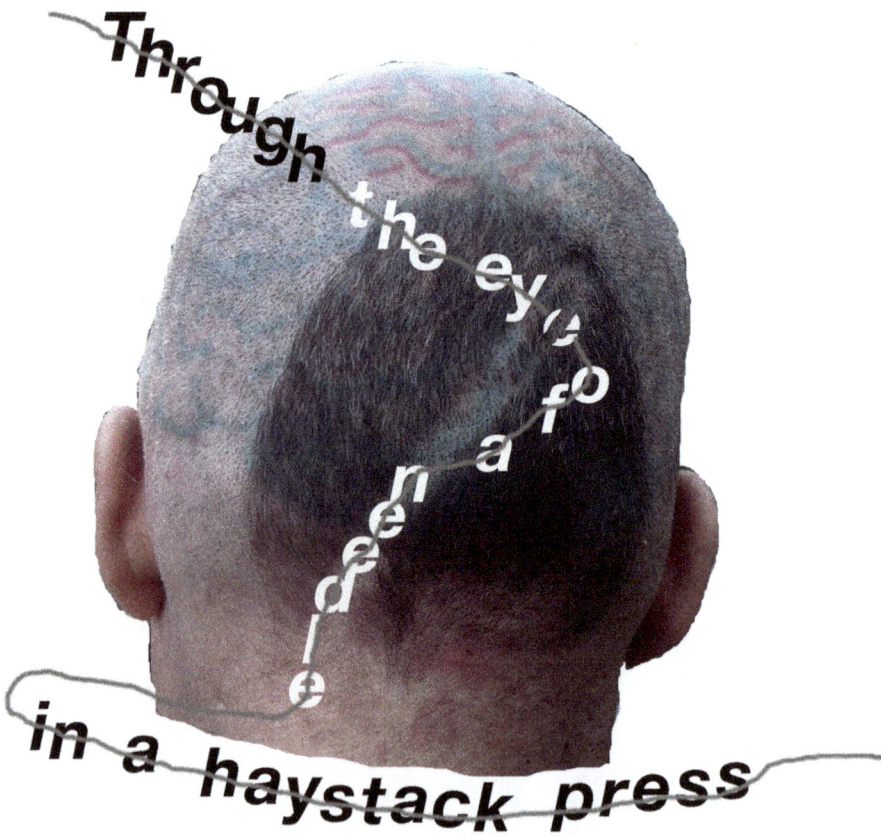

ISBN: 979-8-9871573-3-6

not limited to But (Smattering 2)
Introduction
- tENTATIVELY, a cONVENIENCE
- January, 2024

"not limited to But (Smattering 2)" is the successor to "But not limited to (Smattering 1)". In 2020, I had been invited to be published by an old friend's press. I wrote, designed, & provided all the imagery for "(Smattering 1)" leaving space for the publisher's one page introduction at the beginning, wch I slotted in when I got it. That one page intro was the publisher's sole contribution. He left the actual nuts & bolts of getting the printing done to another old friend, unpd. I left the back cover for old friend 2 to design.

Given that we were all old friends, there was no contract, I took it for granted, erroneously as it turned out, that I would get complimentary copies of the bk that was my creation as the publisher's way of actually doing something. The idea of publishing, as I understand it, is that the publisher picks work deemed to be worthy of widespread distribution, the publisher picks up the bill & pays the creator for their having provided the work. Then both of them receive royalties.

However, in this case, the publisher had a different idea of what constitutes "business". Their idea was that I would do all the work, provide the product, not get any complimentary copies - having to buy them instead. Hence, when I asked to buy 100 of them from the publisher they charged me roughly TWICE what the actual cost was for them. I complained about this both to them & to old friend 2 & the publisher reluctantly refunded me something like $300, still maintaining a sizeable profit for theirself & grumbling like they were somehow doing me a favor.

I later parodied their 'business model' by explaining it thusly: Imagine someone opening a supermarket. They get all the goods to be sold in advance w/o payment, they hire employees to run the supermarket, they, personally, do as little work as possible. A mnth passes & the creditors want to be pd, the employees are expecting their 1st paycheck. The owner of the supermarket announces: "I'm in business to make money for me. Your financial problems are your problem, not mine." & he doesn't pay anybody. If he manages to keep the supermarket going it's only b/c he finds a new supplier & new employees.

The 'publisher' is NOT a businessman, they're just someone who rips off their friends. I unpublished the bk, no doubt surprising the 'publisher', making it so that they can't make any further money off of my work. Fortunately, I still have 80+ copies left if anyone wants one.

SO, "not limited to But (Smattering 2)" is both a continuation of "(Smattering 1)" & a partial replacement for it online. After I wrote & published & unpublished "(Smattering 1)" I eventually realized there were some shortcomings in it. The most important one was a small section missing from the "Collector's Item" section about my rubber stamps, I'd accidentally left out my Japanese stamp & some txt preceding

& following it. I'd also forgotten to color in some of the stamps. I've since corrected this by working the improved "Collector's Item" essay into a new bk "Rubber Stamps vs World Dominators!!!!!". I'd also left out 2 photos from the "Pictogrameting" section so I've decided to include the new improved version here. The "Air Drops" section was slightly deficient so, once again, I've added to it & included it here. Other than those 2 examples, everything here is new. The emphasis, as w/ "(Smattering 1)", is on the visual, txt is kept to a simple explanatory minimum.

I'm extremely prolific. It's no exaggeration to say that I have 10s of thousands &, probably, hundreds of thousands of works that cd be published as a part of this series. As such, what's presented here is just a smattering. Nonetheless, it's unlikely that there'll be more Smatterings to come, I have too many other bks to write. Taken together, the 2 Smatterings aren't really as superficial as the word "smattering" implies. They give a pretty good idea of the variety of my graphic work.

Bone of Contention
With Matching Air Conditioner,
To Go

NOTE

The blank pages in this book are an integral part
of its design. They are included to provide breaks
in the sequence of photographs.

TOLSON, MICHAEL FREDRICK. 2813 Greenlawn Road 21207. 9/4/53. 71. Favorite: Country Joe and the Fish. "Nascent, orthopteran, subaist, luxated oleographic, turgid, libraic, excogitate, excentric, hydrophytic, creepy, hilarsia, magnetize."

IN SEPTEMBER OF 1969, WHEN I WAS 16, IT WAS TIME FOR ME TO WRITE MY HIGH SCHOOL YRBK SELF-DESCRIPTION. I CHOSE TO WRITE A HIGHLY ABSTRACT & ENCODED ENTRY THAT CONSISTED OF ADJECTIVE, ADJECTIVE, NOUN, VERB; ADJECTIVE, ADJECTIVE, NOUN, VERB; ADJECTIVE, ADJECTIVE, ADJECTIVE, NOUN, VERB. LOOKING AT IT NOW, "LABAIC" DOESN'T SEEM LIKE A NOUN. WHATEVER. I HAD TO GO THRU A LARGE PORTION OF MY DICTIONARY TO FIND WORDS THAT FIT THE DESIRED PATTERN.

THE BEGINNING OF EACH WORD, GOING BACKWARDS, HAD TO SPELL "MICHAEL TOLSON". NOTE THE ENCIRCLING ABOVE. 3 LETTERS IN FROM THE BACK, AGAIN GOING BACKWARDS, HAD TO SPELL "IS STRAIGHT". NOTE THE ENCIRCLING BELOW. THESE ENCIRCLINGS WERE PROVIDED BY KENT BYE WHEN HE SHOT FOOTAGE OF A SLIDE SHOW OF MINE FOR A DOCUMENTARY ABOUT ME THAT HE DIDN'T FINISH. B/C I WAS AN EXTREMELY SKINNY LONG-HAIRED GUY, MOST PEOPLE SEEMED TO ASSUME I WAS A SPEED FREAK. THE JOKE WAS ON THEM.

I'D KNOWN ABOUT JOHN WATERS SINCE I WAS IN HIGH SCHOOL B/C MY GAY FRIEND ALFRED HAD AN OLDER LESBIAN SISTER, LOUISE, WHO WAS PERIPHERALLY ASSOCIATED W/ THE WATERS SCENE. I MET WATERS FOR THE 1ST TIME AT A PARTY AT MARY THE BARTENDER'S PLACE IN FELL'S POINT IN LATE 1972. WATERS WAS STILL MAKING 16MM FILMS THEN. I SAW HIS RECENTLY RELEASED "PINK FLAMINGOES" AROUND THE SAME TIME AT SHRIVER HALL ON THE JOHNS HOPKINS UNIVERSITY CAMPUS.

TO SAY THAT I WAS BLOWN AWAY WD BE AN UNDERSTATEMENT. IT WAS A TRULY FANTASTIC FILM, WHOLEY PERVERSE & BOMBASTIC. I LOVED IT. I WAS ALSO SO INEXPERIENCED THAT I DIDN'T IMMEDIATELY REALIZE THAT DIVINE WAS A DRAG QUEEN. WATERS' NEXT FILM WAS "FEMALE TROUBLE". READING SOMEWHERE THAT HE WAS DOING A CASTING-CALL FOR THAT I TOOK THIS SELFIE IN THE OUTDOOR STAIRWELL OF MY MOM'S HOUSE, WHERE I WAS LIVING, & SENT IT OFF TO PAT MORAN W/ MY PHONE #. IF I EVER GOT A CALL MY MOM WD'VE ANSWERED IT & GOTTEN RID OF PAT PDQ.

1976

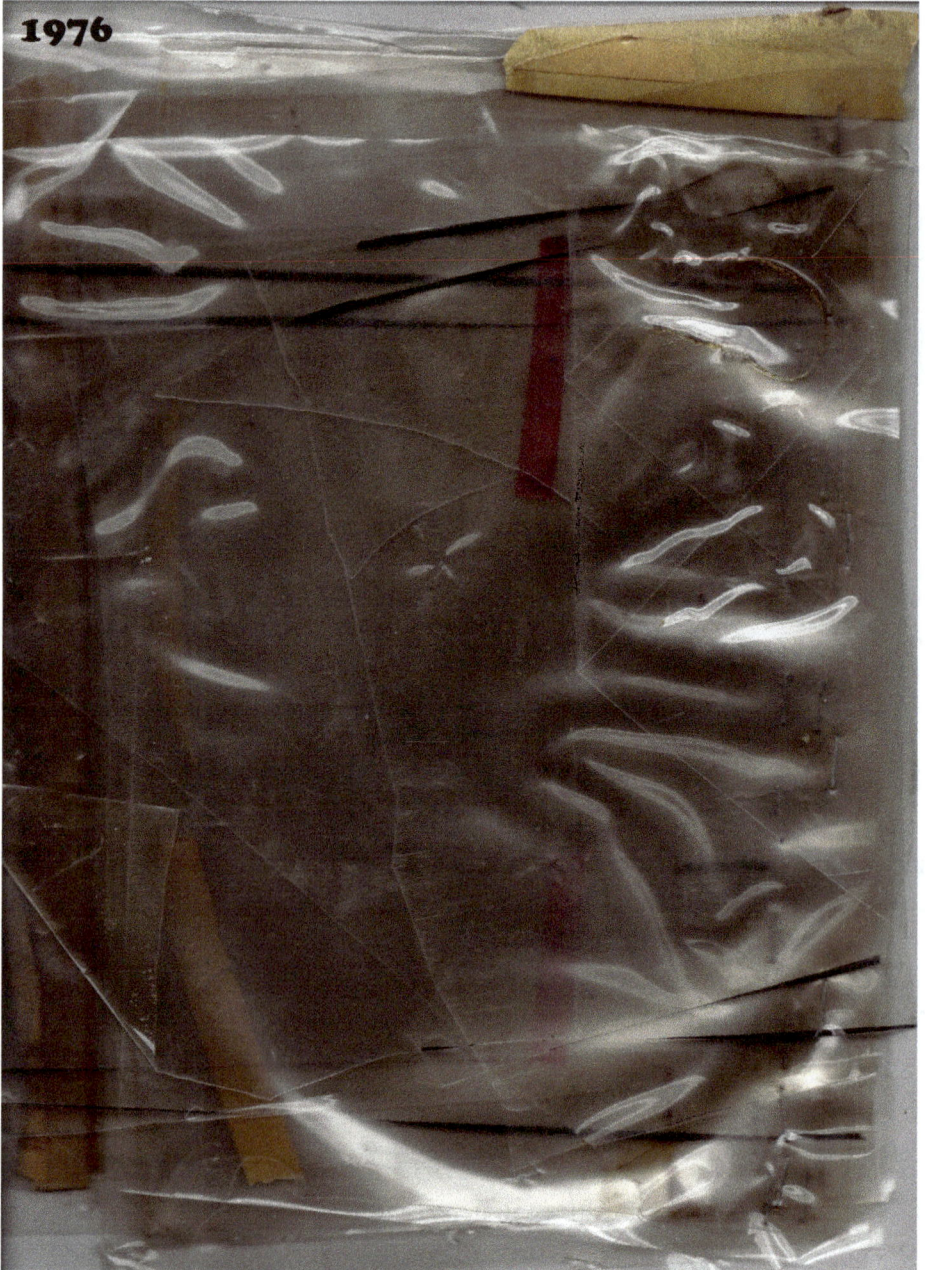

1975-1976 WAS A PARTICULARLY FERTILE TIME FOR ME FOR
EXPERIMENTAL WRITING. IT WAS WHEN I WROTE MY 1ST BK
"T HE BK, T HE REFERENT 4 WCH CONSISTS OF, T HE
TRANSPARENT PUNCH-OUTS FROM A LETTER/WHATEVER
STENCIL". THE BK, PUBLISHED IN 1977, DIDN'T HAVE THE
TITLE ON IT ANYWHERE. THIS WAS A BK OF ALL
TRANSPARENCIES THAT I MADE AROUND THE SAME TIME.

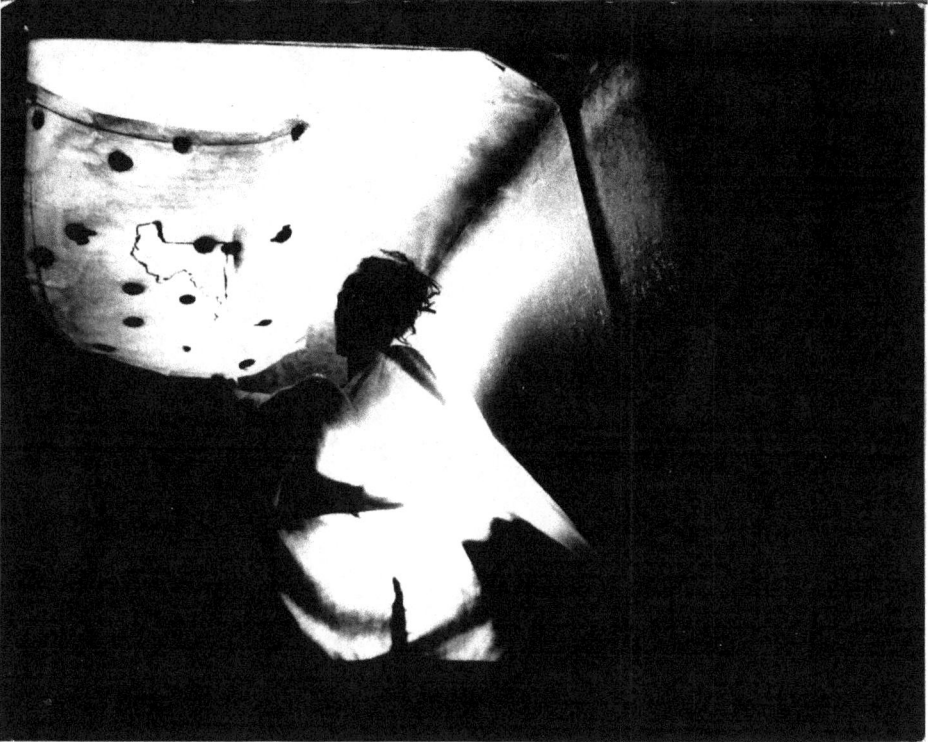

THE WAY I REMEMBER THIS, WCH IS, ADMITTEDLY, NOT VERY CLEARLY, IS THAT I RETURNED FROM MY 1ST TRIP TO EUROPE & MOVED IN W/ MY GIRLFRIEND IN A MANSION THAT HAD BEEN BROKEN INTO APARTMENTS. AS A PRESENT TO HER, I MADE 10 "STATES OF MIND": PERHAPS 2' X 3' PIECES OF PAPER THAT I'D PAINTED AN OUTLINE OF MARYLAND ON, THE STATE THAT WE LIVED IN, & PUT SPRAY-PAINT POLKA-DOTS ON. I GAVE EACH OF THEM A WIRE FRAME ON THE BACK, PROBABLY MADE FROM CLOTHES HANGERS & THEN HAD SOMETHING ATTACHED TO THOSE FRAMES TO ENABLE ME TO HANG THESE STATES OF MIND FROM THE CEILING. THEY WERE HUNG COVERING THE CEILING IN SUCH A WAY THAT ANY BREEZE WD MAKE THEM GENTLY SPIN. I PROBABLY INSTALLED IT FOR HER WHILE SHE WAS AT WORK SO SHE'D BE SURPRISED WHEN SHE GOT HOME. I DON'T REMEMBER HER LIKING IT. I DON'T REMEMBER WHAT SHE DID W/ IT, I IMAGINE SHE DESTROYED IT. APPARENTLY, I SAVED ONE OF THEM & INSTALLED IT AT A PLACE THAT I LIVED AT W/O HER. THE ABOVE SEEMS TO BE A PHOTO OF ME W/ THE 'SURVIVOR'.

MY 3RD FILM & 4TH MOVIE WAS CALLED "GHOST, A PROJECTIONIST'S NIGHTMARE" & WAS DESIGNED TO FALL APART WHILE BEING PROJECTED. THIS WAS AIDED BY DELIBERATELY FLIMSY SPLICES & OTHER SUCH NO-NOS OF FILM PRODUCTION. THIS SCREEN WAS MADE IN A SIMILAR SPIRIT FOR THE FILM TO BE PROJECTED ON TO MAKE IT ALL-BUT-INCOMPREHENSIBLE.

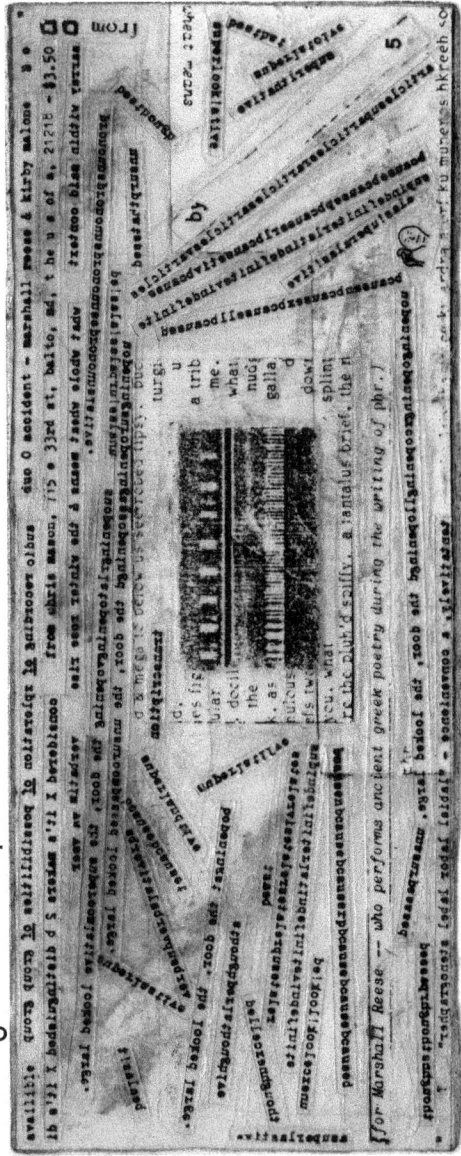

CHRIS MASON FOUNDED
WIDEMOUTH TPAES IN
JANUARY, 1979. THE 1ST
TAPE HE PUBLISHED WAS
"DUOOACCIDENT", A
RECORDING OF A SOUND
POETRY READING AT STATION
HILL PRESS IN UPSTATE
NEW YORK BY CHRIS'S
COLLABORATORS & FRIENDS
MARSHALL REESE & KIRBY
MALONE. ALL 3 OF THEM
WERE IN A GROUP CALLED
"COACCIDENT" - HENCE
THE "DUOOACCIDENT"
NAME FOR THIS DUET
VERSION.

CHRIS ASKED ME TO WRITE A
REVIEW OF THIS TAPE FOR
THE MARYLAND WRITERS'
COUNCIL'S SMALL PERIODICAL
CALLED "HARD CRABS".
THIS IMAGE IS OF THAT
REVIEW. THE CENTRAL
RECTANGLE IS OF A PIECE OF
AUDIO TAPE THAT I DEVELOPED
TO REVEAL THE MAGNETIZED
PORTIONS.

THE REVIEW IS VERY METICULOUSLY DONE & INCLUDES
LIPSTICK TRACES FROM KIRBY & MARSHALL. THIS WAS THE
VERY 1ST REVIEW I EVER WROTE. OBVIOUSLY, IT DOESN'T
SERVE THE GENERAL REVIEW FUNCTION OF TELLING THE
READER ABOUT A PRODUCT - BUT IT DOES GET ACROSS THE SPIRIT.

1979

THESE PHOTOS WERE TAKEN BY ONE OF MY OLDEST
COLLABORATORS, **PAULA GILLEN.** I DON'T KNOW WHO
PROPOSED MY PLACING THE LIGHT METER CLOSE TO MY
GENITALS BUT IT WAS PROBABLY ME. THOSE WERE THE DAYS
WHEM I CD DO SOMETHING LIKE THIS & HAVE THE
PHOTOGRAPHER GO ALONG W/ IT RECOGNIZING IT AS A GOOD
IMAGE. THESE DAYS, I SUSPECT THE PHOTOGRAPHER WD RECOIL
FROM ME AS IF I WERE A PERVERT. THE UNDERSHIRT WAS
SOMETHING I GOT AT A THRIFT STORE. THE TELEPHONE PILLOW
HAS "VD-RADIO" STENCILLED ON IT. THAT'S A REFERENCE TO
THE 'TELEPHONE STN' THAT I WAS CORUNNING AT THE TIME.
THAT DATES THIS AS IN THE 2ND HALF OF 1979. I'M HAPPY TO
SAY THAT PAULA & I ARE STILL FRIENDS 45 YRS LATER & SHE'S
GAME TO TAKE CREDIT FOR THESE PHOTOS. SOME FRIENDS OF
MINE FROM THOSE DAYS ARE PROBABLY TOO BOURGEOIS TO BE
ANYTHING BUT EMBARRASSED BY SUCH THINGS.

This is another one of **Paula Gillen**'s photos, probably taken the same day, definitely taken in the same School 33 studio. Unlike the last 2 pictures, Paula provided the costume. I've always thought of it as a "toreador" outfit but I don't really know if it's that or a "matador" one or even if there's any difference between the 2. At any rate, I seem to be taking 'the chair by its horns'. I imagine Paula made this oversized chair but maybe another artist at School 33 did & Paula just commandeered it. Whatever the case, I find my profile & overall bearing to be quite 'heroic' don't you?

1979

I'M NOT SURE THAT ALL OF **PAULA GILLEN'S** PHOTOS HAVE TITLES. I THINK OF THIS ONE AS PART OF THE "GROWING PAINS" SERIES & PAULA'S LABELLED IT "CRACKED". I THINK OF IT MORE AS "CREATION MYTH". THE THING I'M WEARING ON MY CHEST IS MY "SALAD DRESSING" - FRAME OF REFERENCE SHAPES W/ BUTTONS ON THEM LINKED TOGETHER BY A DIFFERENT FRAME OF REFERENCE SHAPE W/ BUTTON-HOLES AT EITHER END.

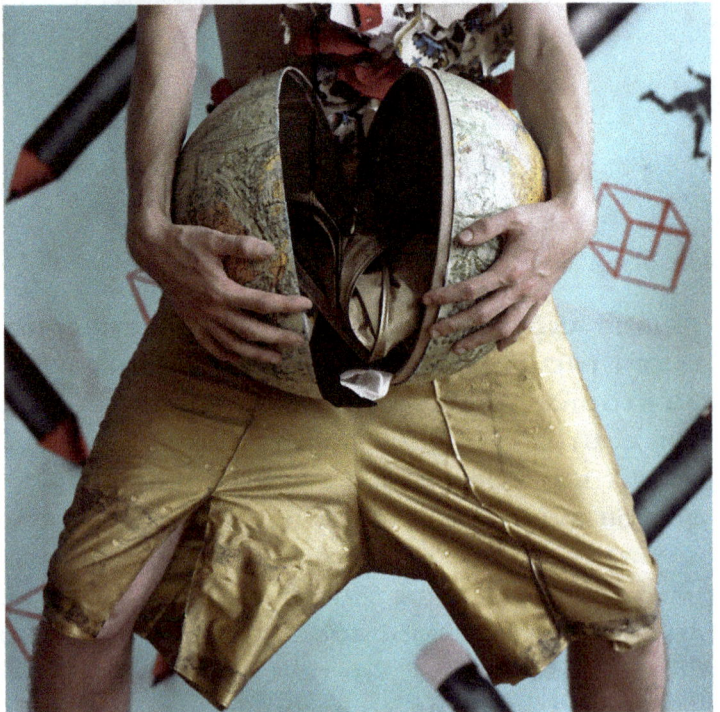

The International Festival of Disappearing Art(s)

BALTiMORE

APRIL 24-28 1980

donation: $3.00 for one night, $10.00 for five nights.

performances

Batto-Wash
1/2 Japanese
CoAccident
Tina Darragh
Stan Edmister
HOPCAS (Hopkins Conceptual Arts Society)

Krononautic Society
Shop Girls
The Tinklers

Beth Anderson — NY
pablo & Theatre Education Center, Inc.

Ron Silliman · SF
Toronto Research Group · Canada
steve mccaffery & bpNichol
P. Clive Fencott · England
Katalin Ladik · Yugoslavia
Greta Monach · Netherlands

recorded schedule: call
☎ (301) 962-0210
April 24-28 only

Sound Poetry
Mad Science
Investigative Music
Folk Math
Film & Video
Intermediate Performance

April 26
8pm
Corpus Christi
Basement
1400 block
W. M. Royal

April 26
12 noon
Our Saviour Lutheran Church
33rd St. & The Alameda
2pm
Rash Field...Inner Harbor

April 25 & 27
7pm
School 33
Art Center
1427
Light St.
(# 64 bus)

April 24 & 28
7pm
Breakall/Noos
Coffeehouse
428
East 31st St.

School 33 is sponsored by
MACAC & NEA

presented by the Merzaum Collective's
Desire Productions

☎ (301) 889-5839   ☎ (301) 889-2519   ☎ (301) 659-7218

film & video

BOMB (Baltimore Oblivion Marching Band)
Carolee Schneemann · NY
The Residents · SF
Dur-An-Ki
Carlos da Ponte of Le Plan K · Belgium
Rick Sugden · FL

FROM 1977 TO 1982, THE MERZAUM COLLECTIVE'S
DESIRE PRODUCTIONS PRESENTED AMAZING EVENTS.

nth international Festival of Disappearing Art(s) -- April 24-28, 1980 -- Baltimore -- for info phone:
(301) 889-5839
presented by the Merzaum Collective's Desire Productions
(301) 889-2519
donation: $3/one night -- $10/five nights
(301) 659-7218

EVENT SCHEDULE

THURSDAY, APRIL 24 @7PM --   Bread and Roses Coffeehouse
                              426 E. 31st St.

= sound works by Tina Darragh

= Vermeulen slide-flute concert
  by Greta Monach

= language events and sound & action
  essays by Toronto Research Group

= films: by Carlos da Ponte
         & FUSES by Carolee Schneemann

MONDAY, APRIL 28 @7PM

= 3 Mile Island media residue
  by BOMB

= a performance by The Tinklers

= TJANTING, a reading
  by Ron Silliman

= a videotape of ETHEROGENE
  by Dur-an-ki

School 33 Art Center
(sponsored by MACAC & NEA)
1427 Light Street (bus #64)
(8 blocks south of Inner Harbor)
phone: 396-4641

FRIDAY, APRIL 25 @7PM --

= piano & vocal music
  by Beth Anderson

= HUGH II, an opera
  by P. Clive Fencott

= 3 CoAccidents:
  --Earnest & Frank pod:
    The Future Can Be Simulated
  --THE HUMAN PINATA by Gayle 26/x
  --HARRY & THE HOME-MADE ROBOT
    & other works by Chris Mason

SUNDAY, APRIL 27 @7PM

= Svexner Labs (a CoAccident)
  investigative music by
  Mitchell Pressman
  & Alec Bernstein

= sound poetry performances by
  Katalin Ladik
  & Greta Monach

= A THEATRICAL TRIPTYCH
  by pablo &
  Theatre Education Center, Inc.

SATURDAY, APRIL 26 @12NOON

= BELLTOWER MAYPOLE MUSIC
  by Beth Anderson
@ Our Saviour Lutheran Church
  33rd St. & The Alameda (bus #s 3, 22, 36)

SATURDAY, APRIL 26 @2PM

= 5 VOWELS, a kite sky-text performance
  by Stan Edmister, Kirby Malone & Marshall Reese
  w/vocals by Lisa Land, Fencott, Monach, Mason,
  Ladik & others
@ Rash Field -- Inner Harbor
(co-sponsored by the Maryland Kite Festival)
(rain date: Sunday, Apr. 27, 2pm)

SATURDAY, APRIL 26 @8PM

= music by ½ Japanese
  HOPCAS
  Shop Girls

= films: THIRD REICH 'N ROLL
  by The Residents
  & LIMITS by Rick Sugden

= DULUTH & BOLOGNA
  a night-club act
  by TEC's pablo & Janet Lee Olson

@ Corpus Christi Basement
  1400 blk. of W. Mt. Royal
  (sponsored by Maryland Institute
  of Art's Campus Ministry Office)

MERZAUM'S DESIRE PRODUCTIONS WERE TRULY AMAZING & BROUGHT INTERNATIONAL AVANT-GARDE WORK TO BALTIMORE THAT I WASN'T LIKELY TO WITNESS THERE OTHERWISE. IN THIS CASE, THERE WAS A SPECTACULAR PRESENTATION OF EXPANDED POETRY - INCLUDING SOUND POETRY. IT WAS A PARADISE FOR PEOPLE W/ MY INTERESTS. KATALIN LADIK, A WELL-KNOWN ACTRESS & SOUND POET. HAD COME FROM YUGOSLAVIA. EVEN THO WE DIDN'T KNOW EACH OTHER, SHORTLY BEFORE HER PERFORMACE STARTED SHE HANDED ME A 35MM STILL CAMERA & ASKED ME TO TAKE PICTURES. I DECIDED TO SURPRISE HER & USE A FORMAL PROCEDURE THAT WD BE INTENDED TO HAVE THE FINAL PRODUCT BE A

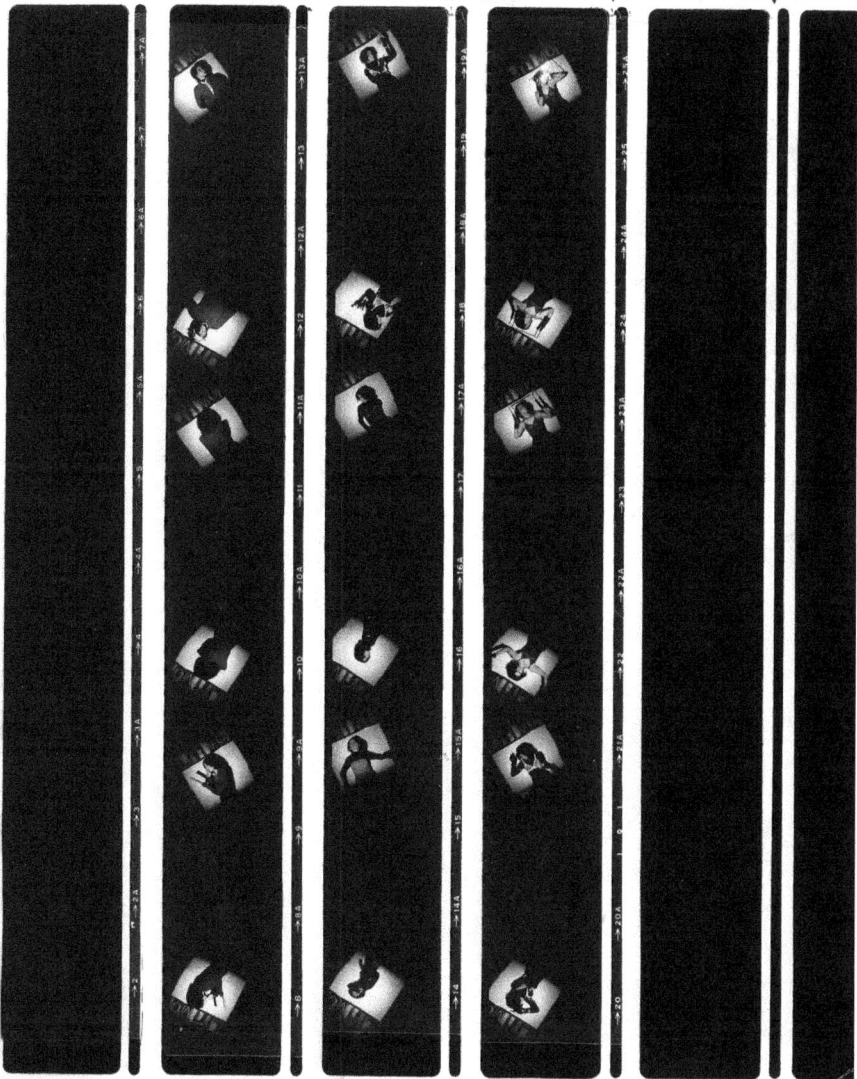

CONTACT SHEET. THE ABOVE IS THE RESULT (ON ITS SIDE).
I DON'T REALLY REMEMBER ANY MORE BUT WHAT MUST'VE
HAPPENED IS THAT SHE TOOK HER CAMERA BACK & I KEPT
THE ROLL OF FILM SO I CD PROCESS IT & PRINT IT AS A
CONTACT SHEET. NO DOUBT, THE INTENTION WAS TO THEN
SEND THE RESULT TO HER. I MADE THE CONTACT SHEET &
THEN BLEW IT UP TO 3 TIMES ITS SIZE: THREE 8X10S TAPED
TOGETHER. DESPITE MY USUAL RELIABILITY, SOMEHOW, I
DIDN'T GET THIS TO HER.

1980.04.27

FESTIVAL DELLA PAROLA

Venezia Poesia '97
Budapesten

MEGHÍVÓ

A Francia Intézet, az Olasz Intézet, a MU Színház és a Magyar Műhely Munkacsoportja szeretettel meghívja a VENEZIA•POESIA '97 BUDAPESTEN rendezvényeire.

INVITATION

L'Institut Français, L'Institut Italien, le Theatre MU et le Groupe de Travail Magyar Műhely (atelier hongrois) vous invitent a assister aux deux soirees VENEZIA•POESIA '97 a BUDAPEST.

INVITO

L'Istituto francese in Ungheria, L'Istituto Italiano di Cultura per L'Ungheria, il Teatro MU e la collettiva del Magyar Műhely ha il piacere di invitare la S.V. agli eventi del festival VENEZIA•POESIA '97 a BUDAPEST.

17 YRS LATER, LADIK & I WERE SCHEDULED TO PERFORM IN THE SAME SOUND POETRY FESTIVAL IN BUDAPEST SO I TOOK THE LARGER PRINT OF THE CONTACT SHEET W/ ME TO GIVE HER.

1980.04.27

Veneziapoesia '97 Budapesten
————————————————————————

1997. Július 9

1. <u>Bevezető</u> (Nagy?)   — 1 mikroport
                                — fény felülről és elölről (mozogni fog)

2. <u>Nagy – Montels</u>: Prae-részletek (felolvasás)
                                — 2 álló mikrofon
                                — felülről és elölről megvilágitva
                                — utca-effektus is lehet

3. <u>Tompa Mária</u> (bemutatja Kovács Zsolt)
                                — dia-vetitő + mikroport + hangkazetta
                                — világitás tompitott

4. <u>Ladik Katalin</u> (bemutatja L. Simon László)
                                — 1 álló mikrofon + 1 mikroport + hangkazetta
                                — ő és a hátsó nagy állvány élesen megvilágitva

5. <u>Vass Tibor</u> (bemutatja Kovács Zsolt)
                                — videókazetta + hangkazetta + 1 mikrofon (álló, v. mikr
                                — sötét terem

6. <u>Szkárosi Endre</u> (bemutatja Kovács Zsolt)
                                — hangkazetta + 2 mikrofon (dobogó vagy asztal)
                                —fény:

7. <u>Mészáros Ottó</u> (bemutatja L. Simon László)
                                —

8. <u>John Gian – Rita Degi Esposti</u> (bemutatja Szkárosi Endre)
                                — 2 álló mikrofon + Hnagkazetta + dia
                                — éles szembe fény

9. <u>Laurence Borrel – Bruno Montels – Nagy Pál</u> (Montelst és Borellt bemutatja Nagy P.)
                                — videó
                                — sötét terem

10. <u>Ghera</u> (bemutatja Sőrés Zsolt)
                                —

11. <u>Angela Idealism</u> (bemutatja Sőrés Zsolt)
                                —

12. <u>tENTATIVELY</u> (bemutatja Sőrés Zsolt)
                                —

13. <u>Szegedy-Maszák Zoltán</u> (bemutatja L. Simon László)
                                — számitógép + Képmagnók + vetitő
                                — 1 mikroport Szegedynek
                  Sz.-M. Zoltán bemutatja tanitványait

SO, I GOT TO BUDAPEST & KATALIN LADIK & I WERE BOTH
WAITING TO DO OUR SOUNDCHECKS & I STARTED WALKING
TOWARD HER TO SHOW HER THE CONTACT SHEET. & I
STOPPED B/C SHE LOOKED TOO FORBIDDING. I'D HEARD SHE'S
A FAMOUS ACTRESS SO I DIDN'T WANT TO BOTHER HER.

Maryland
Writers' Council
1110 St. Paul St.
Baltimore, MD. 21202

SIGNATURES: Baltimore Artists' Books

Sue Abramson

Nancy Andrews

Nancy Bell

Bonnie Bonnell

The Dork Brothers

Mindell Dubansky

David Fair

Dorothy Ford

Cathy Gayhardt

Paula Gillen

Susan Gossling

Alfred Harris

Martha Jackson

Marshall Reese

Doug Retzler/Sumu Pretzler

Richard & the Krononautic Organism

Yoko Sampson

Tom Martin

Nora Ligorano

Kirby Malone

Ro Malone

Lisa Mandle

Michael Frederick Tolson ktp

Joyce Scott

STE Ǝ -V SQUE Ǝ -G

Laurie Stepp

Rick Sugden

The Tinklers

Ruth Turner

Gayle 26/X

Lee Warren

Grace Zaccardi

typography by David Beaudoin

This event is made possible, in part, by grants from the National Endowment for the Arts and the Maryland State Arts Council, with assistance from the Maryland Writers Council.

Desire Productions events are part of the International Festival of Disappearing Art(s)

For information write: Desire Productions, 3022 Abell Avenue Baltimore, MD 21218

IN 1981, I WAS INVITED TO BE PART OF AN ARTISTS BOOKS
EXHIBIT AT THE ENOCH PRATT FREE LIBRARY, CENTRAL
BRANCH. PARTICIPATING IN A ARTISTS BOOKS SHOW WAS
EXCITING B/C ARTISTS BOOKS WERE STILL VERY NEW IN MY
ENVIRONMENT. I EXHIBITED MY 1ST BK , WCH HAD A
SECTION THAT DISSOLVED IN WATER, SO I HAD THAT BK OPEN
TO THAT PAGE & PLACED IN A GOLDFISH BOWL FILLED W/
WATER.

1981.03.21

Merzaum's Desire Productions and the Enoch Pratt Free Library present an exhibition

SIGNATURES: BALTiMORE ARTISTS' BOOKS

21 March through 2 May 1981

Hands-On Demonstration - 11:30 am

An Introduction to Artists' Books - 2:00 pm a talk by Peter Frank associate editor of Art Express

Reception - 3:00 pm

March 21 Opening Day

for information (301) 889-5839 ☎

at the Enoch Pratt Free Library 400 Cathedral St. Baltimore

THE OTHER BK I EXHIBITED WAS CALLED "HOSPITAL ART THERAPY BOOK 4 ALFRED". IT HAD BEEN A BLANK HARDBACK BK THAT I'D RIPPED THE PAGES OF & MARKED W/ BLACK MARKER. THE RESULT WAS A SORTOF ABSTRACT EXPRESSIONIST FLIPBK. THEN THERE WAS THE "IRENE DOGMATIC PAPER DOLL BOOK" THAT WAS THE 1ST MAIL ART PUBLICATION I CONTRIUTED TO. THERE WAS A CATALOG, TOO, FOR WCH EVERYONE CONTRIBUTED A PAGE. MY PAGE WAS EXTREMELY METICULOUS. THE POSTER WAS BY RO MALONE.

1981.03.21

REMO UNDERWATER

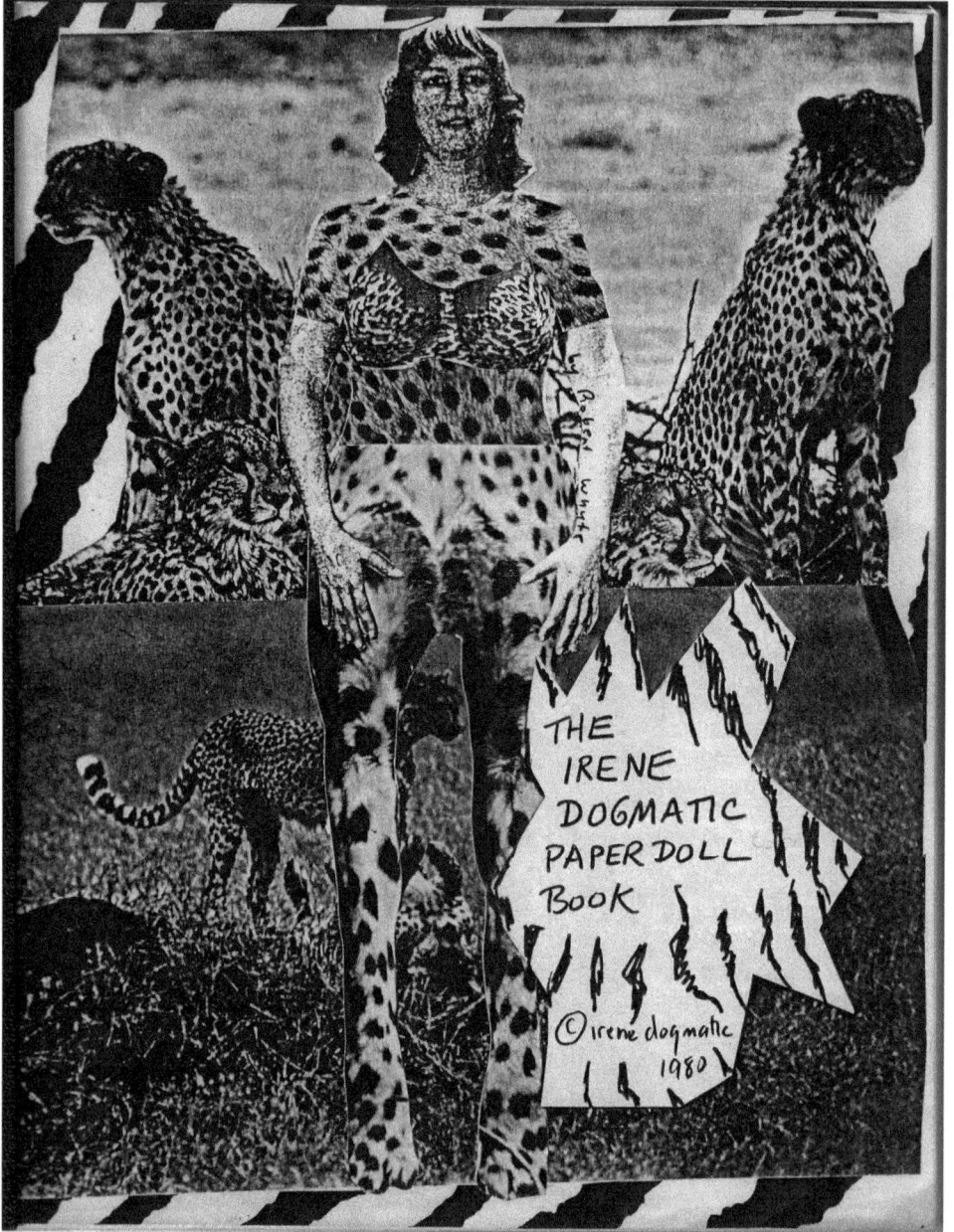

THE
IRENE
DOGMATIC
PAPER DOLL
BOOK

©irene dogmatic
1980

MT-
BALTIMORE

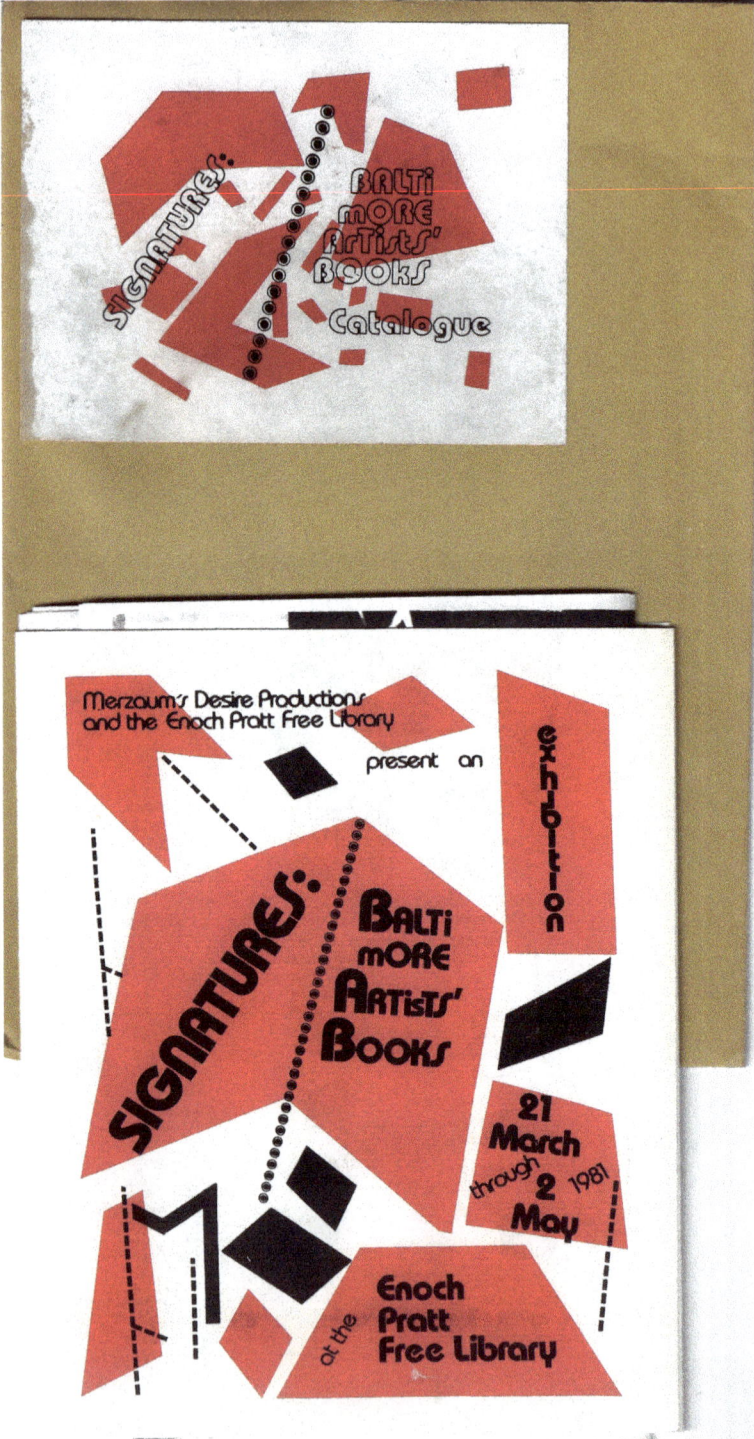

SIGNATURES:
BALTimORE ARTiSTS' BOOKS
Catalogue

Merzaum's Desire Productions
and the Enoch Pratt Free Library

present an

exhibition

SIGNATURES: BALTimORE ARTiSTS' BOOKS

21 March through 2 May 1981

at the Enoch Pratt Free Library

T HE RE
T HE NON-

Michael

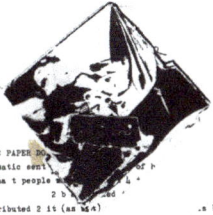

(THE IRENE DOGMATIC PAPER DO

    irene dogmatic sent   of h

requesting t ha t people m   4

        2 b   ed

    i contributed 2 it (as M t)   s book show

as an example of cooperative pos   book making)

T HE BOOK * WHICH CONSISTS OF
T HE REFERENT & THE
T HE NON-MATERIALIZED PUNCH-OU

LETTER/WHATEVER STENCIL

Michael

(THE IRENE DOGMATIC PAPER DO
    irene dogmatic sent   f h
requesting t ha t people   4
      2 b   ed
    i contributed 2 it (as M t)   s book show
as an example of cooperative pos   book making)

FROM

X Art X

Freder

    self
    he doll
    &2 a book.
    include it in th
    l communications

1981.03.21

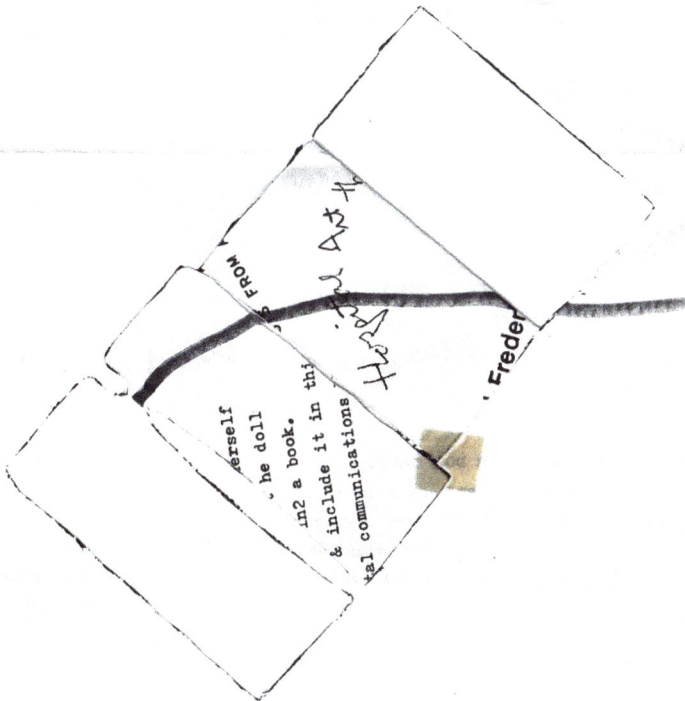

1981

TWO FRIENDS OF MINE, CASANDRA VON RINTELN & VALERIE
FAVAZZA, ARE SHOWN ABOVE BATHING IN A TUB FULL OF RIT
DYE. VALERIE, IN PARTICULAR, WAS INCLINED TO WEAR ALL
BLACK MORE OFTEN THAN NOT SO I PROPOSED TO BOTH OF
THEM THAT THEY SHD 'GO ALL THE WAY' & DYE THEIR SKIN
BLACK TOO. SINCE THEY WERE BOTH GAME FOR WEIRDNESS,
THEY DECIDED TO TRY. THEY DIDN'T HURT THEMSELVES
(ALTHOUGH I STILL WDN'T RECOMMEND THIS!} BUT THEIR
SKIN DIDN'T TURN BLACK. INSTEAD, THEY WERE PURPLE.
I DON'T REMEMBER HOW LONG IT LASTED, AT LEAST A WK.

THIS IS ONE OF MY FAVORITE PHOTOS EVER TAKEN OF ME.
SALLY HUTCHINS TOOK IT & SHE USED A TECHNIQUE IN
DEVELOPING WHERE SHE JUST SPLATTERED THE
DEVELOPER ACROSS THE PAPER IN THE DARKROOM. NICE!

I DON'T KNOW WHAT YR THESE 2 PICTURES WERE TAKEN. I THINK THE 2ND ONE MIGHT BE FROM 1985. HERE I AM VISITING MY FAMILY ON XMAS. MY FAMILY WAS VERY CONSERVATIVE & I VERY MUCH DIDN'T BELONG. THE FIGURE AT THE BOTTOM IS MY "DEPRESSED SANTA" THAT I MADE TO BRING THERE.

I THINK NANCY ANDREWS PROBABLY TOOK THESE SLIDES FOR ME. I HAD MOVED INTO SOUTH BALTIMORE WHERE THE LEVELS OF HATRED & DEPRAVITY WERE HIGHER THAN ANYWHERE I'D LIVED BEFORE. THESE PICTURES WERE ALL DOUBLE EXPOSURES SO THAT I CD BE SHOWN WEARING 2 OUTFITS PER IMAGE. IN THIS CASE, I'M WEARING TRANSPARENT CLOTHES & NAKED UNDERNEATH. HARD THO IT MAY BE TO BELIEVE, I ACTUALLY DRESSED LIKE THIS OUT ON THE STREETS. TO SAY THAT THE RECEPTION OF THE AVERAGE HIGHLY DEBASED SOUTH BALTIMORON OF ME WAS HOSTILE WD BE A GRAND UNDERSTATEMENT. I KNOW THAT AT LEAST ONE OF THE LOCAL COSTRUCTION WORKERS TOOK IT FOR GRANTED THAT I HAD A GUN HIDDEN - B/C HOW ELSE CD I DARE TO BE SO OUTRAGEOUS?! IN THE FOLLOWING PICTURES THERE'S A PAIR OF PANTS MADE FROM A SOFTSHELL GUITAR CASE. IN ANOTHER PICTURE I'M WEARING STRIPED TOOTHPASTE ON MY EYEBROWS.

1982

FOTO(S) TAKEN BY: NANCY ANDREWS

sensitively, a convenience — RIGHT

LEFT — HANNAH AVINA

FOTO(S) CONCEIVED OF BY: sensitively, a convenience

THIS IS A STEREO PHOTO, MEANT TO BE SEEN W/ A STEREO VIEWER. IT MIGHT WORK IF YOU JUST CROSS YOUR EYES. CASANDRA'S ON THE LEFT, I'M ON THE RIGHT. WE'RE WEARING THE SAME CLOTHES & IN THE SAME SHOT. THE IDEA WAS THAT WE'D MERGE INTO ONE PERSON. WE WERE VERY ROMANTIC.

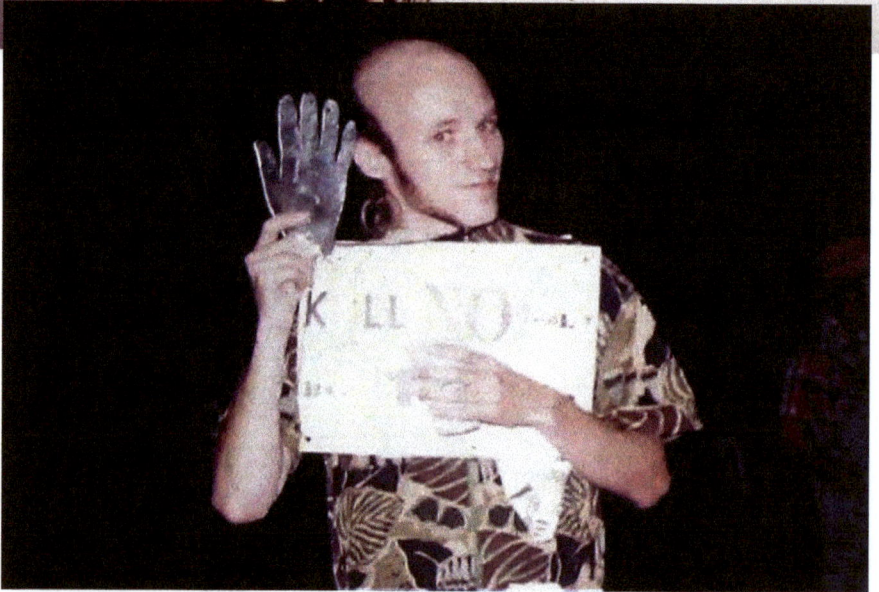

IN SEPTEMBER, 1982, MY GIRLFRIEND, CASANDRA, & I DROVE TO
CHICAGO FOR THE 2ND CHURCH OF THE SUBGENIUS
CONVENTION. I'D BEEN INVITED BY REVEREND STERNO TO PLAY
"ANTI-MUSIC" W/ DRZ FOR "BOB" SO I CAME PREPARED W/ SOME
ELCTRICAL DEVICES TO TURN THE AMPS ON & OFF. THAT WASN'T
WHAT THEY HAD IN MIND. THE CAMOU I'M WEARING WAS A
LETTER FROM STERNO.

1983.01

THIS IS PART OF A SERIES OF PHOTOS TAKEN AT MY REQUEST
BY MY FRIEND SALLY HUTCHINS TO ACCOMPANY A
DAILY NEWSPAPER ARTICLE ABOUT A RADIO PROGRAM I
WAS ABOUT TO AIR. IN RETROSPECT IT'S AMAZING THAT THE
DAILY PAPER WENT ALONG W/ THE SIMILAR IMAGE THEY
CHOSE..

u as hereX invited/considered 2 b
an honorary member of <u>OLFACTORIES ORGANIZED</u>.
this olfactory organ as 4 t he purpose
of conducting R&D in odiferous areas.
4 further info contact:
tentatively, a convenience
(301)0576-0586
box 382, cr(ater) balto, MD, 21203, US Ⓐ

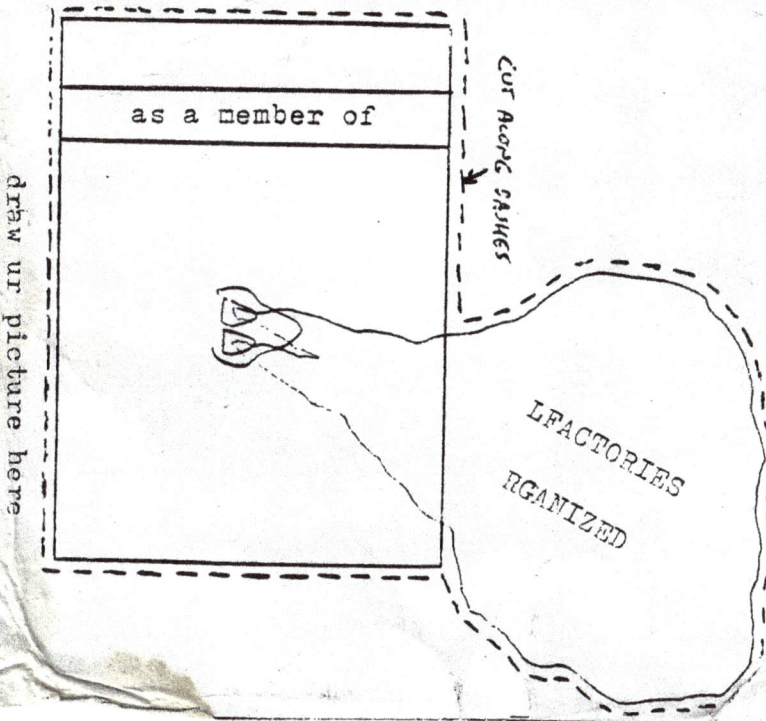

as a member of

draw ur picture here

CUT ALONG DASHES

LFACTORIES
RGANIZED

IT WAS PROBABLY IN 1983 THAT I FOUNDED OLFACTORIES
ORHANIZED, THE GROUP WHOSE LOGO WAS 2 "O"S MADE
SOMEWHAT TRIANGULAR TO REPRESENT NOSTRILS. THE
PURPOSE OF THE GROUP WAS TO SMELL THINGS & IT WAS
MY INTENTION TO ORGANIZE FIELD TRIPS TO DO THAT.
THE ABOVE WAS BOTH AN INVITE & AN ID CARD. THE
RECIPIENT WAS TO FILL IN THEIR NAME & DRAW THEIR FACE
AROUND THE NOSTRILS. WHETHER ANYONE EVER DID THAT IS
DOUBTFUL.

1983

I, OF COURSE, STARTED SPREADING THE WORD TO MY VARIOUS
COLLEAGUES. I CD USUALY COUNT ON AT LEAST ONE NEOIST TO
GET INTO THE SPIRIT OF THE THING. IN THIS CASE, IT WAS ALAN
LORD OF MONTRÉAL. SEE THE NEXT PAGE FOR A LIST OF WHAT
THE ABOVE VIAL CONTAINED.

"SM-L THIS"

CONTENTS:

1) "FROTTAGE" TECHNIQUE (RUBBING) APPLIED TO DIFFERENT PARTS OF MY DIRTY BODY, ROLLING OFF LIKE PUTTY

2) TINY DRIED FECAL SAMPLES

3) GUNK FROM BETWEEN MY TEETH OBTAINED WITH DENTAL FLOSS

4) CLIPPINGS FROM SOCKS IN WHICH I PLACED BITS OF CHEESE (3 DAYS WALKING).

5) SAMPLES OF BLACK DIRT FROM MY TOENAILS

6) THE UBIQUITOUS "ROLLED BALL OF SNOT"

7) EAR WAX

8) APPROPRIATE STUFF CULLED FROM MY NAVEL

BY THE TIME I TOOK THE PHOTOS ON THE PREVIOUS PAGE THE CONTENTS HAD, FOR THE MOST PART, TURNED TO DUST. I REMEMBER THE ORIGINAL ODOR BEING STRONG BUT NOW I DON'T SMELL ANYTHING AT ALL.

THE NEOISTS, PEE ON "BOB"'S HEAD, OLFACTORIES

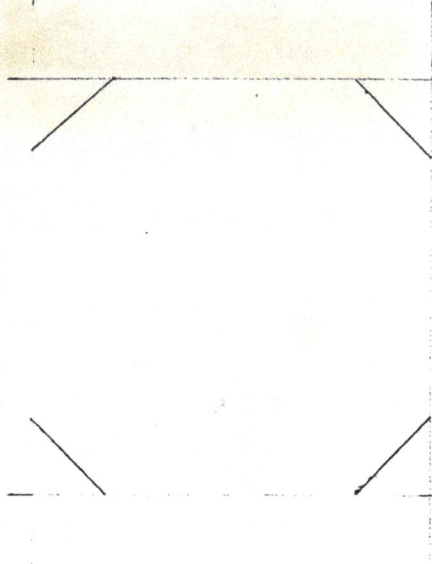

W/ A TIP OF OUR TOPS 2 RAROTONGA, MARIO CAMPA, RICHARD,

ORGANIZED, KODAK, PATA HARI, & tentatively, a convenience -AT LEAST

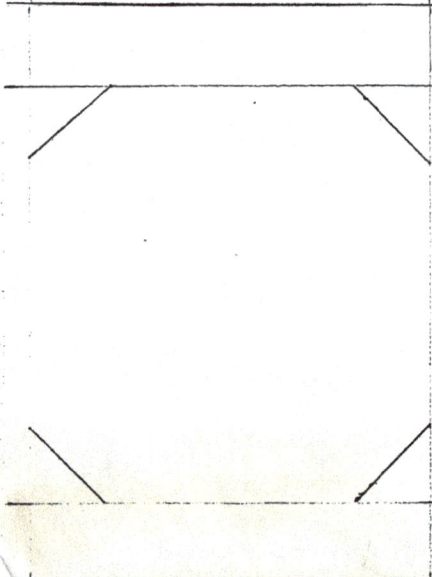

time of pe'e
harmony chant
urself thru
"bob"'s 3rd nostril

LOSS OF SIGNAL

as a member of

OLFACTORIES
ORGANIZED

THE NEOISTS, PEE ON "BOB"'S HEAD, OLFACTORIES

W/ A TIP OF OUR TOPS 2 RAROTONGA, MARIO CAMPA, RICHARD,

ORGANIZED, KODAK, PATA HARI, & tentatively, a convenience -AT LEAST

time of pe'e
harmony chant
urself thru
"bob"'s 3rd nostril

LOSS OF SIGNAL

as a member of

OLFACTORIES
ORGANIZED

I CO-ORGANIZED THE 3RD CHURCH & FOUNDATION OF THE
SUBGENIUS CONVENTION IN BALTIMORE (W/ SAM
FITZSIMMONDS) & ORGANIZED THE 7TH INTERNATIONAL
NEOIST APARTMENT FESTIVAL TO FOLLOW ALMOST
IMMEDIATELY THEREAFTER. FOR THESE 2 GATHERINGS
I MADE THE ABOVE PHOTO HOLDERS. AT THE SUBG EVENT,
AT LEAST, I TOOK PEOPLE'S POLAROIDS, SLOTTED THEM IN,
& GAVE THEM THE RESULT.

Get to Tent
c/o Box 582
Balt., Md.
21203

P.S.– I GOT A YR'S PROBATION (SUPER

Hm, read your "Y" as a "4", eh?

"SUZY"
THE CHINA DOLL
Magic Card
THREE ACTION POSES
NO. 3052   MADE IN TAIWAN

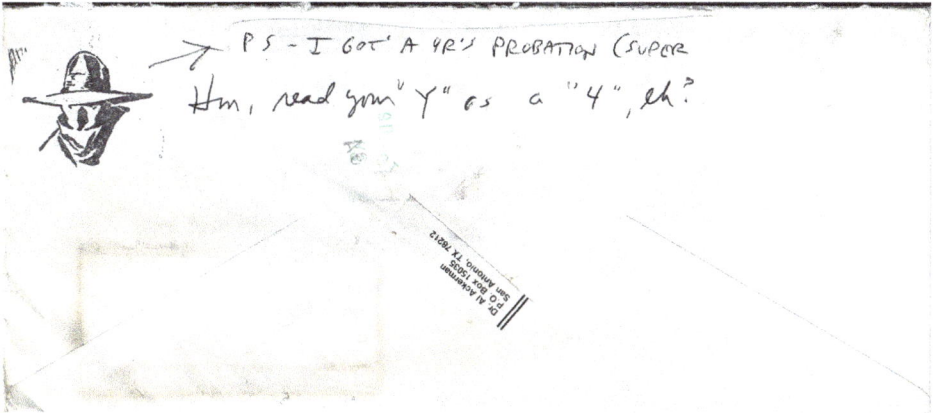

SOME OF THE REASONS WHY I LOVED CORRESPONDING W/
SAL MINEOIST "BLASTER" AL ACKERMAN SO MUCH WAS B/C
HE ALWAYS ENTERED INTO THE SPIRIT OF THINGS, HE ALWAYS
HAD SOME WACKY NEW THING TO SEND ME, & HE WAS
ALWAYS FUNNY.

1983.11.05

PHOTO BY PATTY

INEX,

SLEEZE, LESLIE, LATERAL, BLASTER, LIN   THE
        WHAT,   LAD   SPIEGELMANS, NUNZ, MAPPO.

November 1683 (LUSE(CASFC)

Dear Tent:

Relieved to hear it was a year and not four years! (SUZY - The China Doll
Magic Card is an old jail house toy; guys, particularly the ones in Houston
County, used to slip these in and beat off over them..)

Does your mindless robot mother have an adress? (My mother's favorite
line, whenever I would come up with something really exceptional, was always: "Oh
no! It's my worst nightmare!")

I'll be sending you our secret SHIRKISM Stickers soon. Use them as you
will. Me, I've been brushing up against well-dressed lulus over at the HEB store
and on the street, so that they walk away wearing one of these stickers on their
back. Young matrons wearing those awful blobby white Princess Di stockings
are my favorites.

If you're down in that tunnel anytime soon, keep an eye out for Sewer
Boy. He still lost.

THE SHADOW KNOWS

FROST BROS.
217 EAST HOUSTON STREET
SAN ANTONIO, TEXAS 78205

SAN ANTONIO, TX 782
-PM
24 OCT
1983

USA 20c

DR&Mrs Al Ackerman
P.O. Box 15035
San antonio,Tx. 78212

Al - Hope you can make it ! Niki

Frost Bros.
invites you to
the opening exhibition of
the first fragrance
conceived
as a work of art
by
Niki de Saint Phalle
*Meet this avant garde artist, in person, Friday,
October 28, Cosmetic Shop, Frost's North Star Mall, from 11:00
until 2:00. See examples of her art, on exhibit. Sample her new fragrance. Niki
de Saint Phalle will autograph one of her posters as a gift with any
fragrance purchase. If you wish Niki will give you a signature painting on your
cheek and Frost's will photograph it for you. Her hand-size,
hand-painted Nana spice cookies will be given away,
too! Come and enjoy an art and
fragrance happening.*

SEWER BOY STILL LOST

ON UPPER LEFT HAND CORNER
YOU WILL FIND 3 SLOTS.
INSERT WHITE CARD INTO
EACH SLOT +"WATCH
THE ACTION-TAIWAN"+

NO. 3052   MADE IN TAIWAN

1983

left to rightL Eugenie Vincent, Tim Ore (aka
tENTATIVELY, a cONVENIENCE), Amy Swennerton,
& Chris Mason

additional OO: Jennie Beetz

ONE OF THE ONLY GOOD THINGS ABOUT LIVING WHERE I DID
NEXT TO THE CROSS STREET MARKET IN SOUTH BALTIMORE WAS
THAT I CD SMELL THE MCCORMICK SPiCE FACTORY FROM OVER
HALF A MILE AWAY. FOR THE ONLY FIELD TRIP THAT
OLFACTORIES ORGANIZED WENT ON, WE WENT THERE. THEY
HAD A MODEST SECTION FOR GREETING VISITORS THAT SEEMED TO
MAKE REFERENCE TO WHEN MCCORMICK WAS FOUNDED, IN 1889.

1983

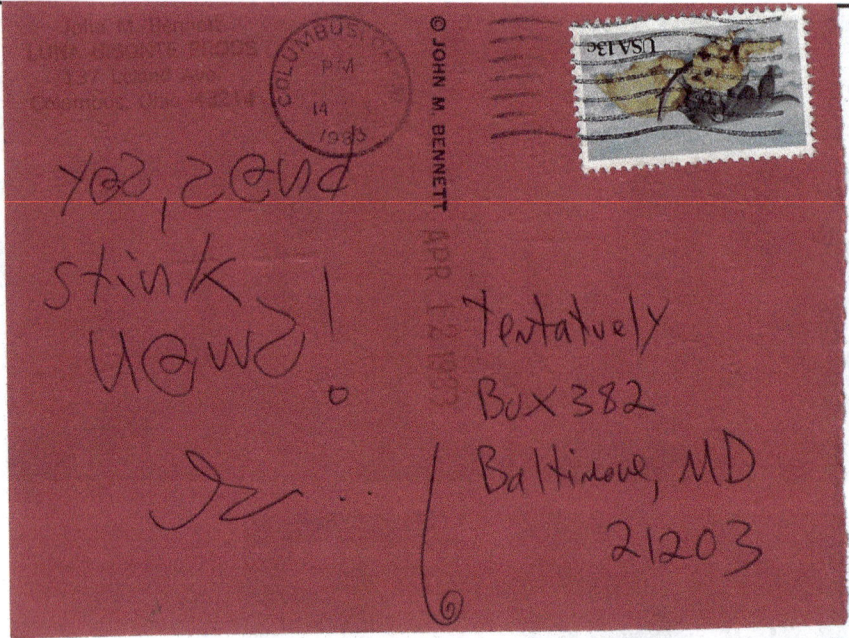

© JOHN M. BENNETT

APR 14 1983

Tentatuely
Box 382
Baltimore, MD
        21203

It took John M. Bennett to rouse the inquiry as to whether there was a connection between Olfactories Organized & the Chicken Movement.

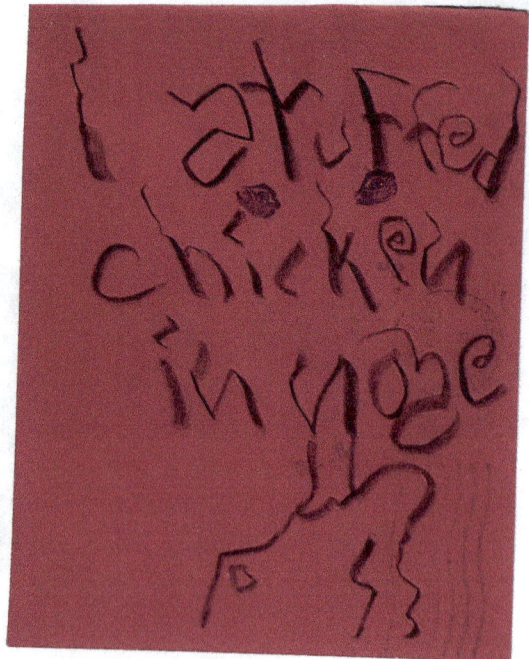

& then there's t he CHICKEN MOVEMENT
about wch it might b important 2 mention
(didn't Istvan Kantor 'v t he job of
breaking t he necks of sickly chicks
w/ black spots on their asses?)
(didn't Ralph Ortiz kill them 4 artistic purposes?)
t he t hearing about chickens BING! raised
from birth 2 death in boxes just large enuf
2 accomodate them at maturity
(didn't Iggy Pop (& geeks in general)
bite off their heads in performance?)
(weren't they executed in at least
2 John Waters films?)
reminds me of hearing t ha t charlie manson.
recently vowed 2 stay in 1 place in his cell.
(didn't Werner Herzog accuse chickens of BING!
t he epidomy of stupidity?)
(didn't Kiki Bonbon kill them during t he
6th APT fest?)
perhaps t he CHICKEN MOVEMENT as a meditative movement
- a meditative bowel movement
- excremeditation in SubG lingo..
(asn't chickens used in voodoo ceremonies?)
& then there's t he curious linking
of t he CHICKEN MOVEMENT w/ OLFACTORIES ORGANIZED..

Emulsively, a Convenition

No, no, I'm not Plas... ...ot sure
he would agree that t... ...anythi...
more important, more c... AS... THE
right now than the THE CHICKEN MOVEMENT.
You may know this, in fact, for all I
know Balto may be the very source of the
emanations and you could very well have
been living w4th CHICKEN CONCEPTS for
quite some time now. And this Olfac.
Org..I was going to cut-out and draw,
butit too has gone through the time
loop and has fled me. Strange thing to
be doing in the midst of THE CHICKEN
MOVEMENT.

MUDJIM

(154 ROGERD-Z, SAN ANTONIO, TX, 78204, US©)

If Found, Please Return To:
BOX 382 CR BALTO MD 21203

t he above as traced from a pc from:
John M. Bennett
LUNA BISONTE PRODS
137 Leland Ave,
Columbus, OH, 43214
US Ⓐ

TIME ORE
BOX 382
CR BALTO
MD.
21203

1984

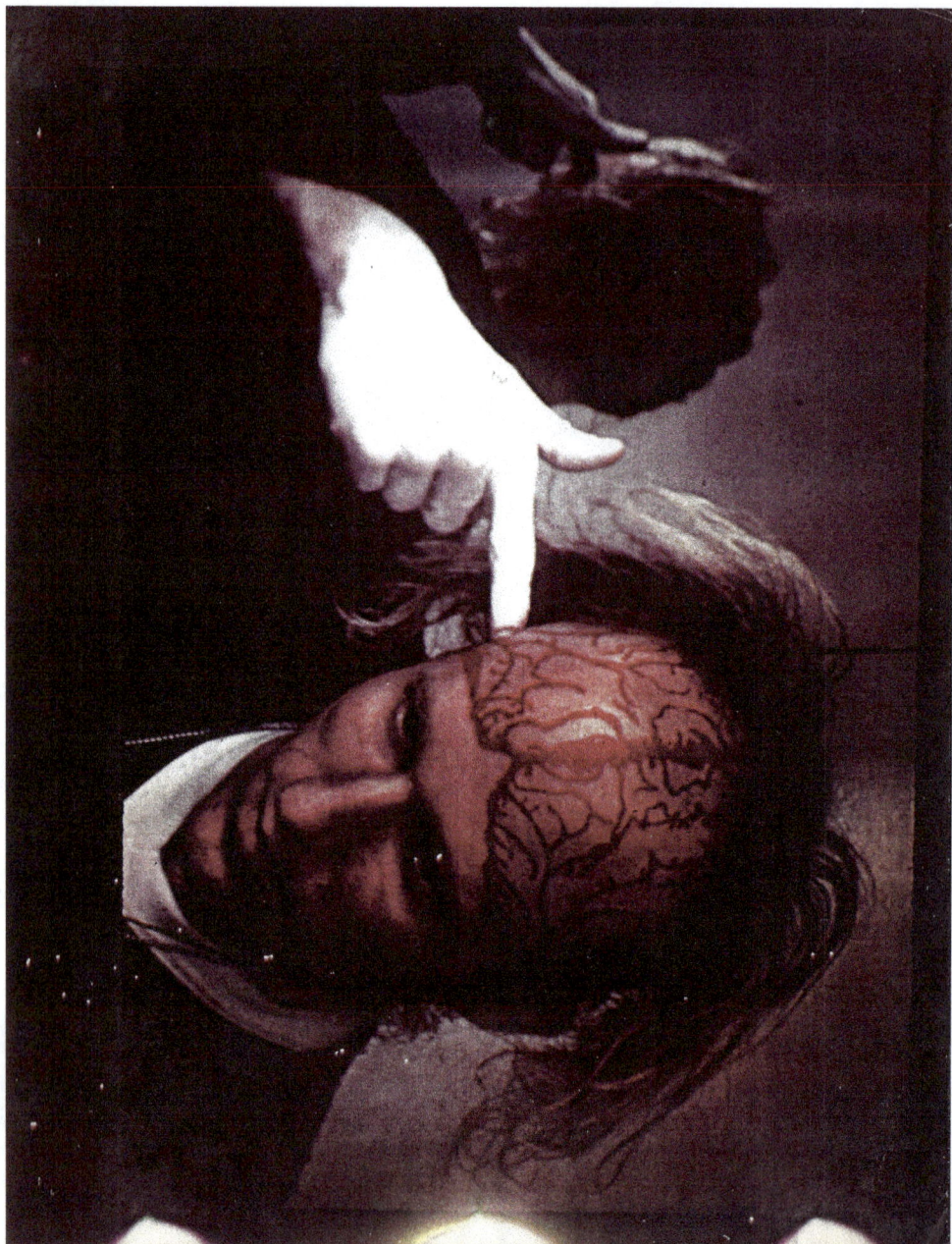

IN 1984 MY GIRLFRIEND, GAIL LITFIN, & I WENT TO LONDON FOR THE 8TH INTERNATIONAL NEOIST APARTMENT FESTIVAL. I'D BEEN THINKING OF GETTING A BRAIN TATTOO ON MY HEAD FOR QUITE SOME TIME BUT HADN'T YET SO I GOT OUR HOST, PETE HOROBIN, TO DRAW THIS ON ME.

GAIL & I WENT TO THE LONDON ZOO WEARING A SHEEP MASK (GAIL) & A GOAT MASK (ME). MANY OF THE PICTURES FROM THIS ARE IN MY BK "HOW TO WRITE A RESUMÉ - VOLUME II: MAKING A GOOD FIRST IMPRESSION" (1988). THIS IS ONE OF THE ONES THAT DIDN'T MAKE IT INTO THAT BK.

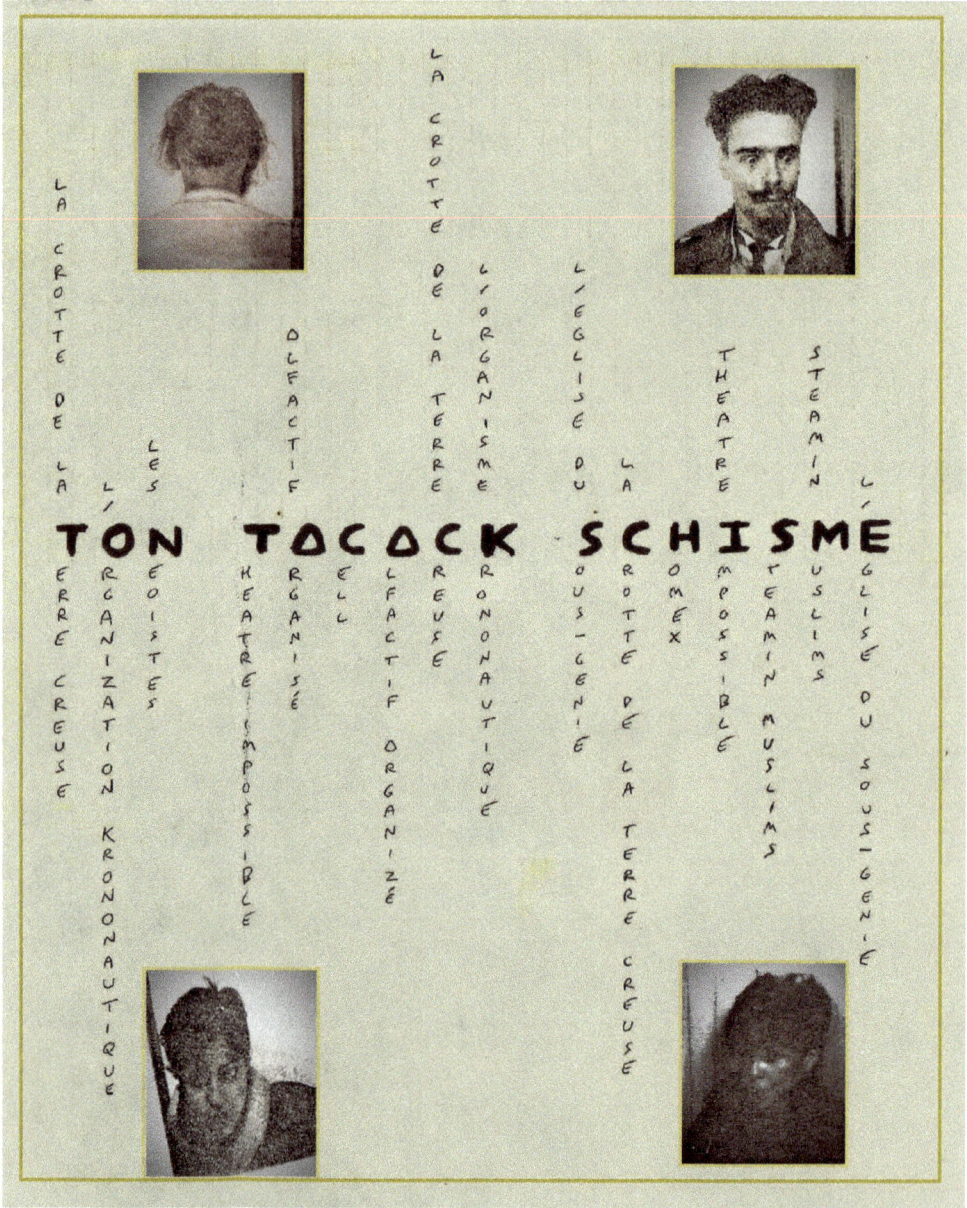

LA CROTTE DE LA TERRE CREUSE

L'ORGANIZATION KRONONONAUTIQUE

LES EGOISTES

OLFACTIF ORGANISÉ

THEATRE (IMPOSSIBLE

ELL

OLFACTIF ORGANIZE

LA CROTTE DE LA TERRE

L'ORGANISME RONONAUTIQUE

L'EGLISE DU SOUS-IGENIE

LA CROTTE DE LA TERRE CREUSE

COMEX

THEATRE IMPOSSIBLE

STEAMIN MUSLIMS

STEAMIN MUSLIMS

L'EGLISE DU SOUS-IGENIE

TON TOCOCK SCHISME

ON THIS SAME TRIP, GAIL & I WERE JOINED BY EUGENIE VINCENT & WE VISITED REINHARDT U. SEVÖL & VIA VIDORAE IN PARIS WHERE WE COFOUNDED A MOVEMENT CALLED "TON TOCOCK SCHISME", THE NAME OF WCH WAS AN ANAGRAM OF SORTS MADE FROM NAMES OF OTHER GROUPS WE WERE INVOLVED IN. NOTE THE INCLUSION OF OLFACTORIES ORGANIZED & THE "O"S BEING SHAPED LIKE NOSTRILS IN "TOCOCK".

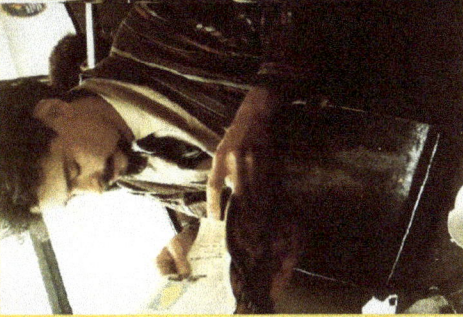

OUR ONLY ACCOMPLISHMENT AS A GROUP (MINUS GAIL & EUGENIE) WAS A FILM CALLED "LES PROMENADES HYSTERIQUES". THE ABOVE PHOTOS ARE A SORTOF TOURIST MEMENTO OF PART OF IT.

1984

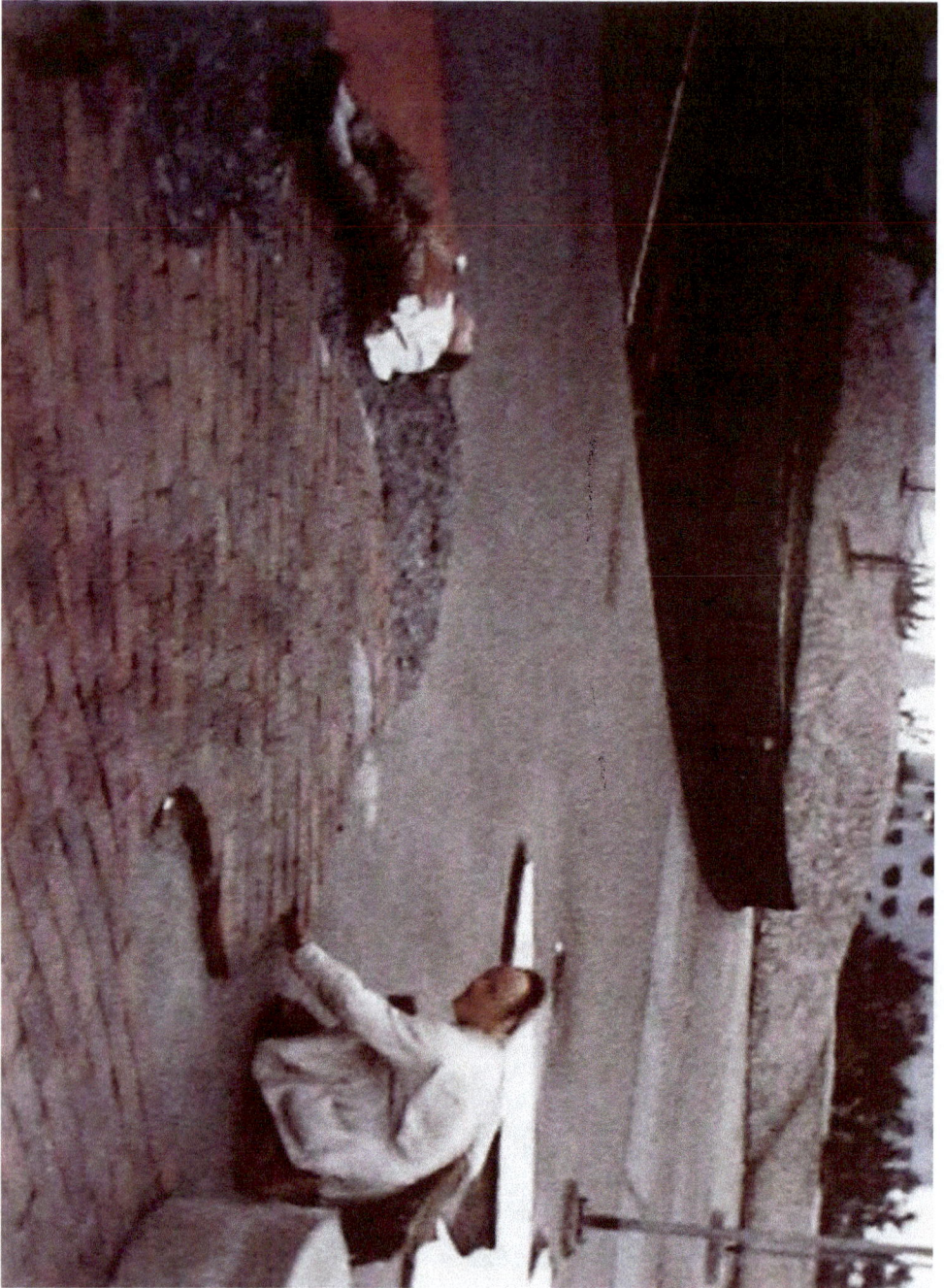

WE DID TAKE A FIELD TRIP TO THE FANTASTIC HOUSING COMPLEX IN NANTERRE CALLED "TOURS NUAGES" (CLOUD TOWERS) (MINUS GAIL). I'M SHOWN HERE W/ EUGENIE. US ARCHITECTS TAKE NOTE. NEOIST ARCHITECT PIERRE ZOVILÉ WROTE HIS ARCHITECT'S THESIS ON THIS HOUSING PROJECT.

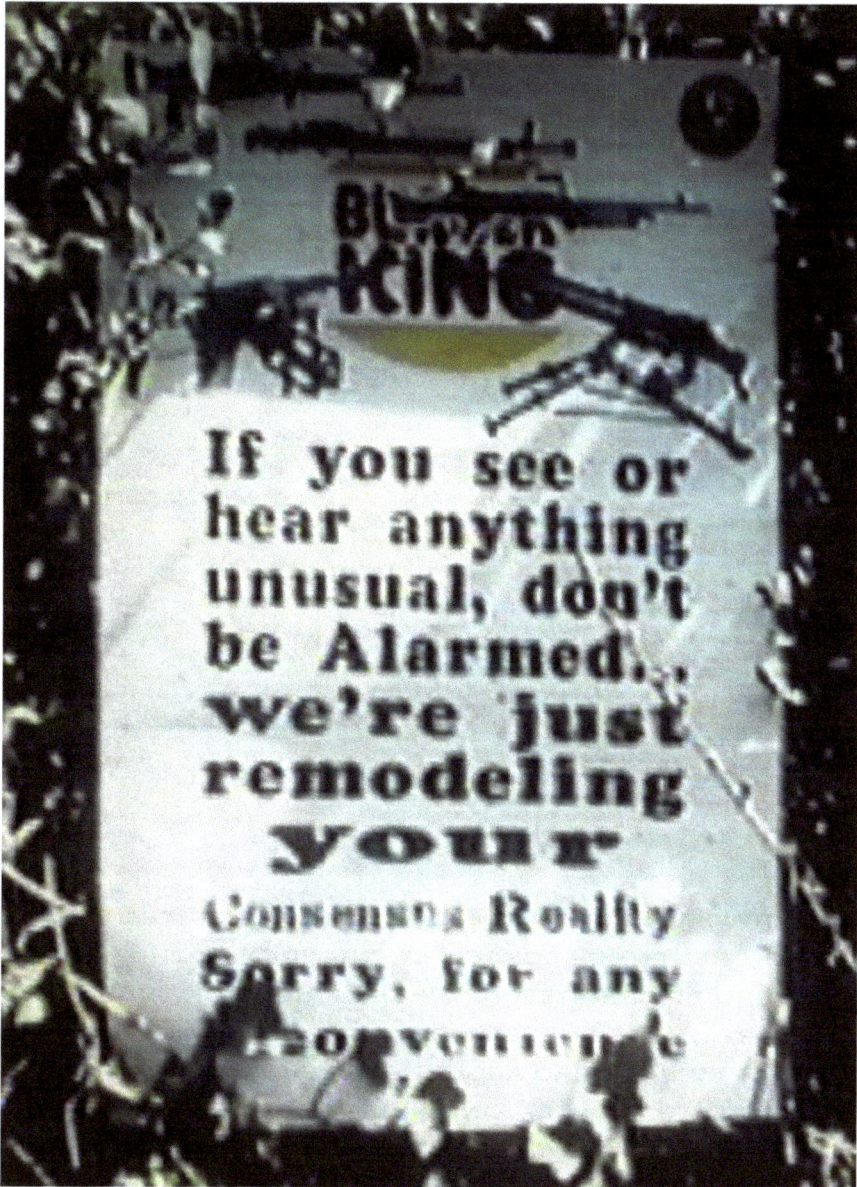

I DON'T KNOW EXACTLY WHEN I MADE THIS SIGN, SOMETIME
BETWEEN 1982 & 1985. MASS SHOOTINGS WERE COMING MORE
& MORE TO MY ATTN. PERHAPS ONE WAS AT A FAST FOOD PLACE.
THEY WERE BEGINNING TO SEEM AS 'AMERICAN AS APPLE PIE',
IN A DYSFUNCTIONAL FAMILY WAY OF COURSE. I TURNED THIS
SIGN INTO A SLIDE THAT I USED TO BEGIN MY 1999 SLIDE SHOW.

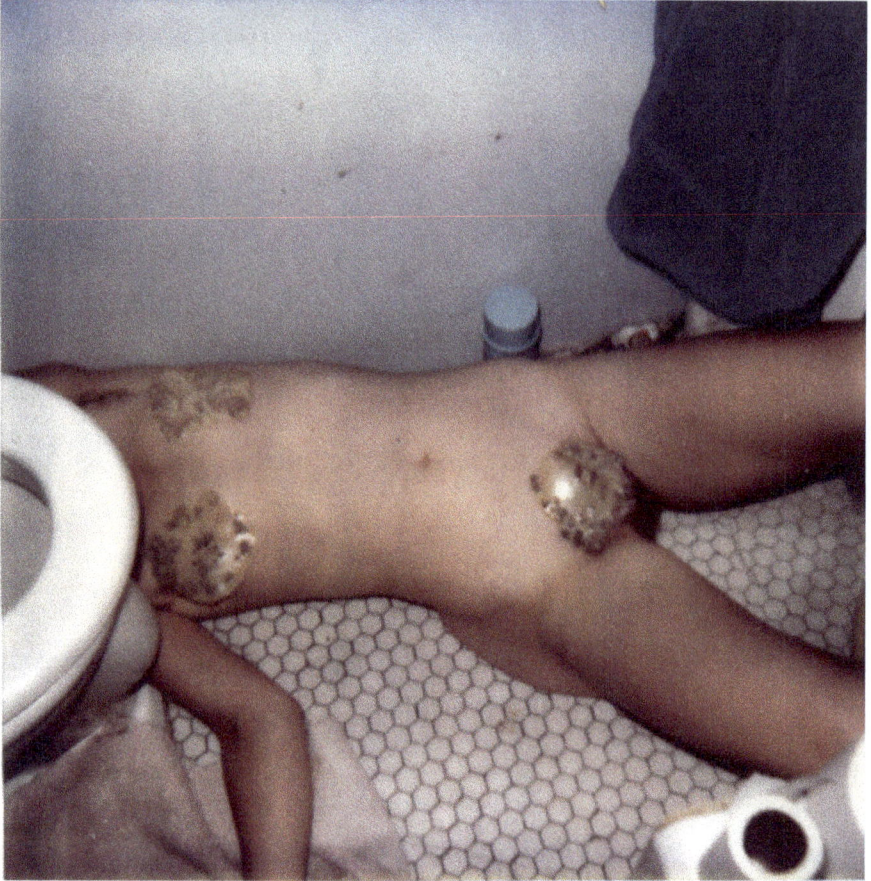

I COLLECT JOKE SHOP GAGS & ONE OF MY FAVORITES IS FAKE
PUKE. IF I REMEMBER CORRECTLY, THE IDEA OF THE "PUKE
BIKINI" SHD BE CREDITED TO MY GIRLFRIEND OF 1985-1986,
JOAN D'ART. HERE SHE IS MODELING IT. I THOUGHT IT WAS
HILARIOUS SO I CARRIED AROUND THIS PICTURE FOR A WHILE
& SHOWED IT TO PEOPLE. ONE NIGHT I SHOWED IT TO A WOMAN
I KNEW A LITTLE IN A BAR, EXPLAINING IT TO HER. SHE THEN
PROCEEDED TO TELL PEOPLE THAT I'D SHOWN HER A PICTURE
OF A "MUTILATED WOMAN". SINCE PEOPLE WERE USUALLY
EAGER TO BELIEVE ANYTHING HATEFUL THAT WAS SD ABOUT
ME THAT JUICY RUMOR WD'VE SPREAD. YOU CAN IMAGINE HOW
MUCH THAT INCREASED MY POPULARITY.

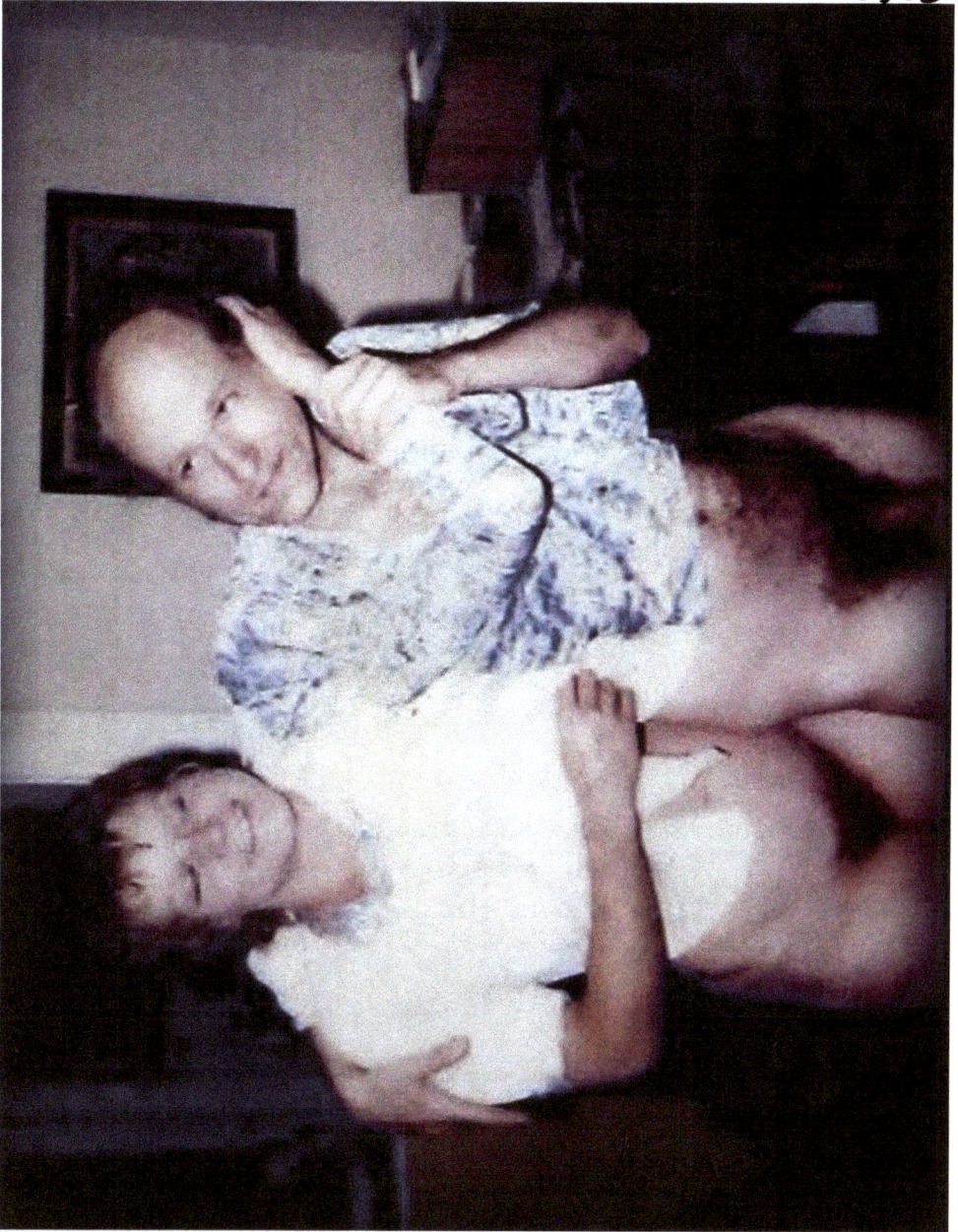

I MADE THIS 'CONJOINED TWINS' SHIRT FOR JOAN & MYSELF BY SEWING TOGETHER 2 SHIRTS. I LOVE THE SLIGHT VISUAL CONFUSION WE CD MAKE W/ IT BY HAVING ONE OF JOAN'S ARMS IN ONE SHIRT'S SLEEVE & THE OTHER IN THE OTHER SHIRT'S SLEEVE.

1985

ANOTHER FAVORITE JOKE SHOP GAG WAS THE PLASTIC BALL &
CHAIN - FAKE, MIND YOU - I HAVE NO MORE DESIRE TO BE
ATTACHED TO A REAL BALL & CHAIN THAN I HAVE A DESIRE TO
PUKE. I WAS WORKING FOR A CHAIN BOOKSTORE AT THE TIME
\WHERE I MORE OR LESS LIKED THE WORK (I LOVE BOOKS!!)
BUT WAS PD VERY LITTLE & WAS OFTEN BORED. I WAS
WORKING TO PAY THE BILLS. NOT EVERYONE HAS THAT
PROBLEM &, UNLESS THEY'RE HOMELESS, I'D SAY THEY'RE
BETTER OFF. SO, I WAS A WAGE SLAVE & I DECIDED TO ACT
ACCORDINGLY BY WEARING THE BALL & CHAIN ON THE JOB.

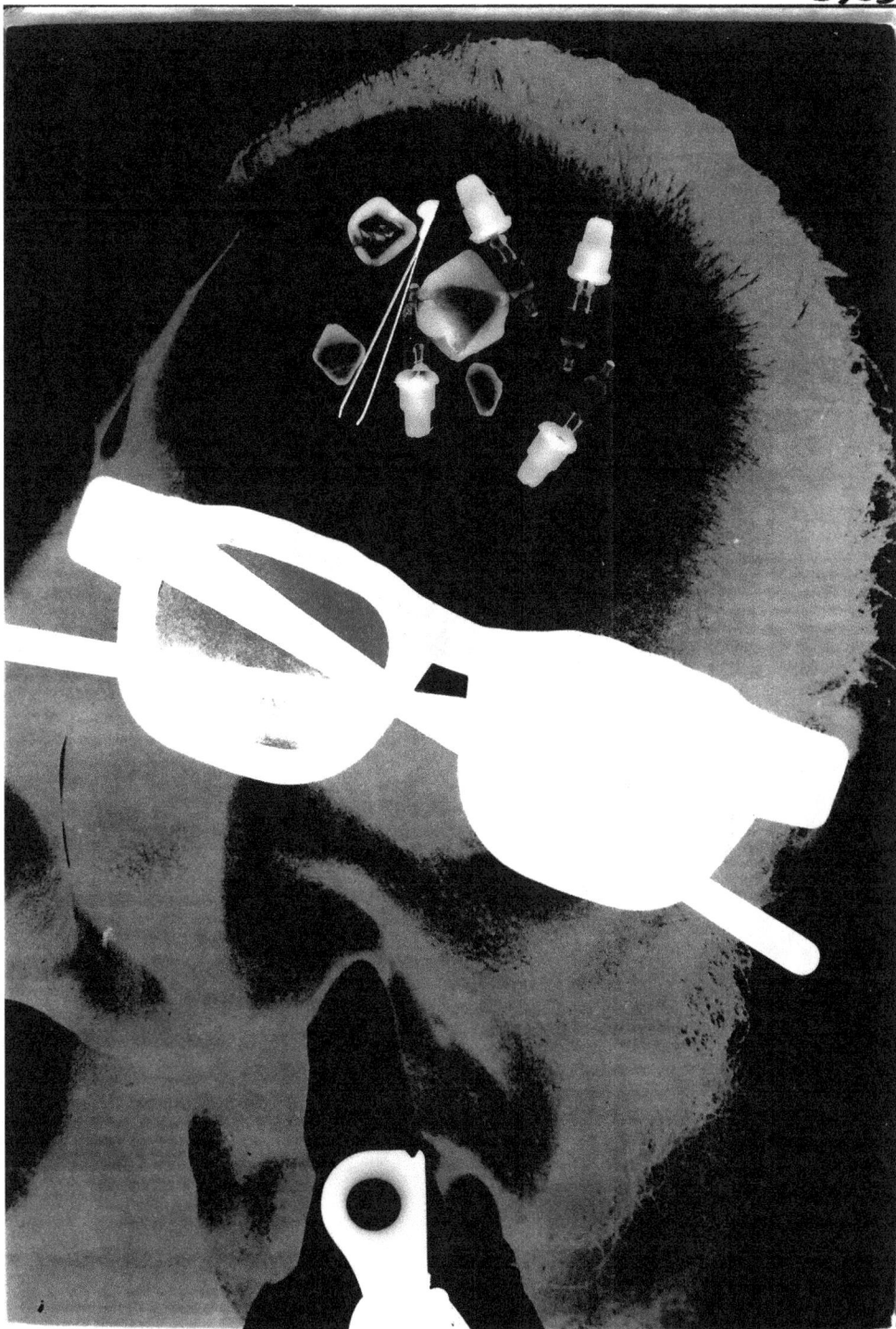

A PHOTOGRAM (OR SCHADOGRAPH OR RAYOGRAM) I MADE USING A
POSITIVE TRANSPARENCY OF MY DISTORTED FACE + OBJECTS.

DATA ATTIC

ceLL e brates

tentatively, a convenience

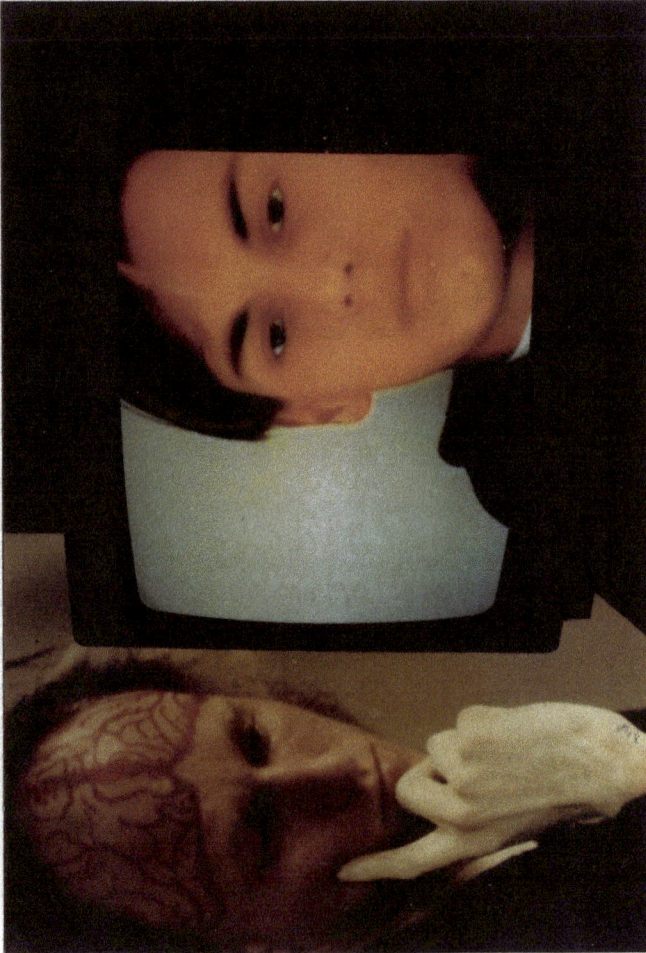

11 5 57 37 UNION STREET DUNDEE DD1 4BS

PETE HOROBIN HAD RELOCATED TO HIS DATA ATTIC IN DUNDEE,
SCOTLAND. MY COLLABORATOR OF THE TIME, JOHN BERNDT,
HAD VISITED HIM THERE. PETE MADE THIS PHOTOCOLLAGE TO
HAVE BOTH OF US BE THERE AT ONCE.

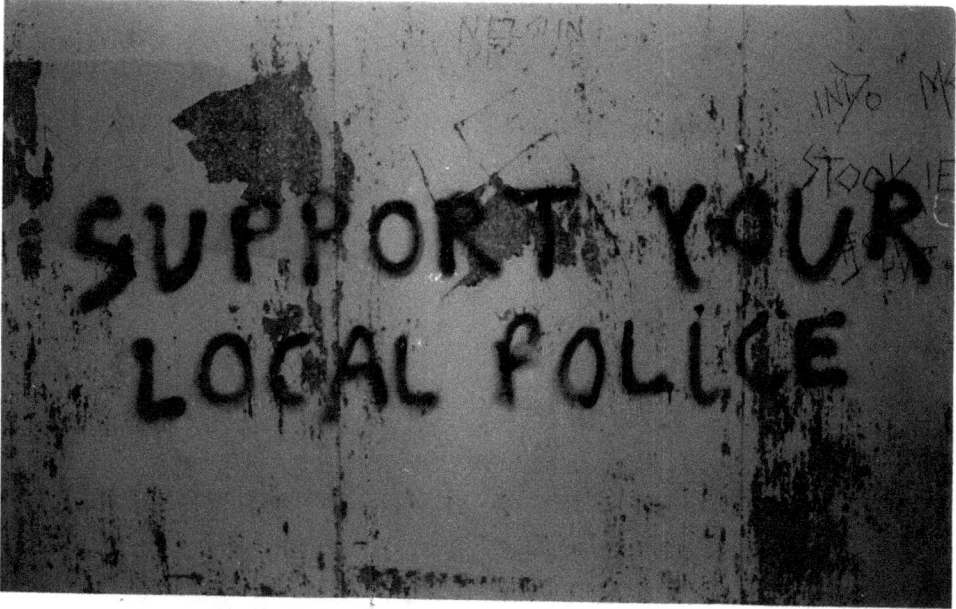

I DID MAKE IT TO DUNDEE THE NEXT YR FOR PETE'S "FESTIVAL OF NON-PARTICIPATION". WHILE THERE, I WENT OUT GRAFFITIING W/ MY FRIEND VEX. SPRAY-PAINTING THE ABOVE WAS ONE OF MY 1ST IDEAS. VEX WAS PERPLEXED, GIVEN THAT GRAFFITIING IS ILLEGAL & THAT THE POLICE REALLY AREN'T USUALLY OUR FRIENDS. I THINK I PROBABLY EXPLAINED HOW FUNNY IT WD BE IF WE GOT CAUGHT PAINTING THIS.

A SIMILAR SENSE OF HUMOR WAS BEHIND THIS NEXT ONE: PAINTING "NO PARKING" ON THE WALL OF A PARKING LOT.

NEOIST HERR STILETTO STUDIOS CAME TO VISIT ME IN BALTIMORE WHERE HE WAS AMUSED TO FIND THAT THE CAT HAD SHAT IN THE BATHTUB IN THE SHAPE OF A COCK & BALLS. I DECIDED THAT THAT WAS A BIT, AHEM, UNSANITARY SO I DECIDED TO PUT A CONDOM ON IT. EITHER STILETTO OR JOHN BERNDT TOOK THE PICTURE.

IN JANUARY OF 1984, I MADE ONE OF MY FAVORITE THINGS:
PANTS MADE ENTIRELY FROM ZIPPERS. IN EARLY 1988, I MADE A
MATCHING JACKET. ON MY 36TH BIRTHDAY, I WASHED & DRIED
THEM FOR THE 1ST TIME. I RECORDED THIS PROCESS. I WAS
PHOTOGRAPHED BY JOHN BERNDT.

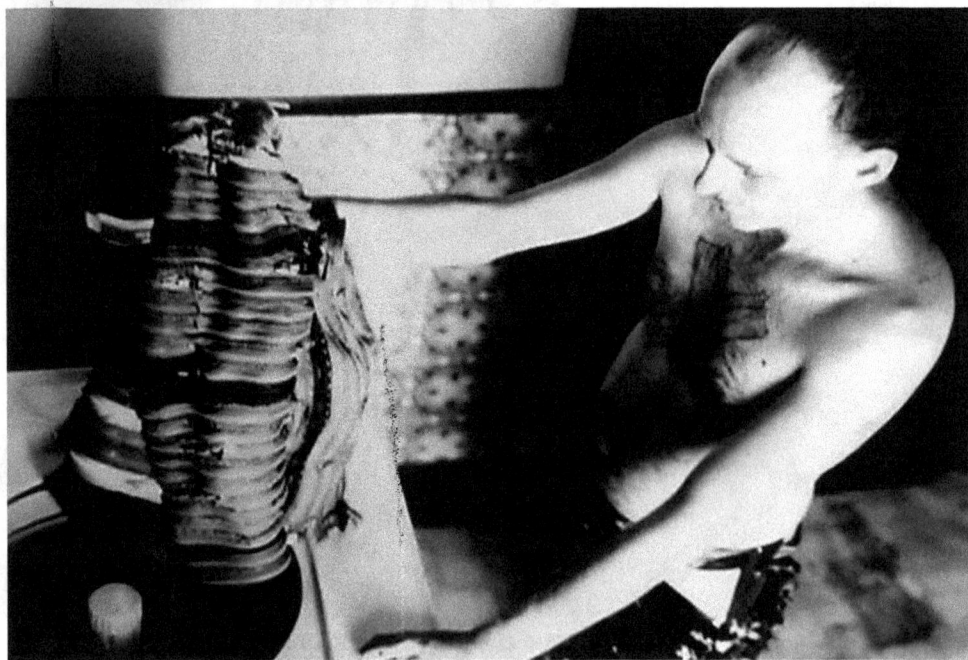

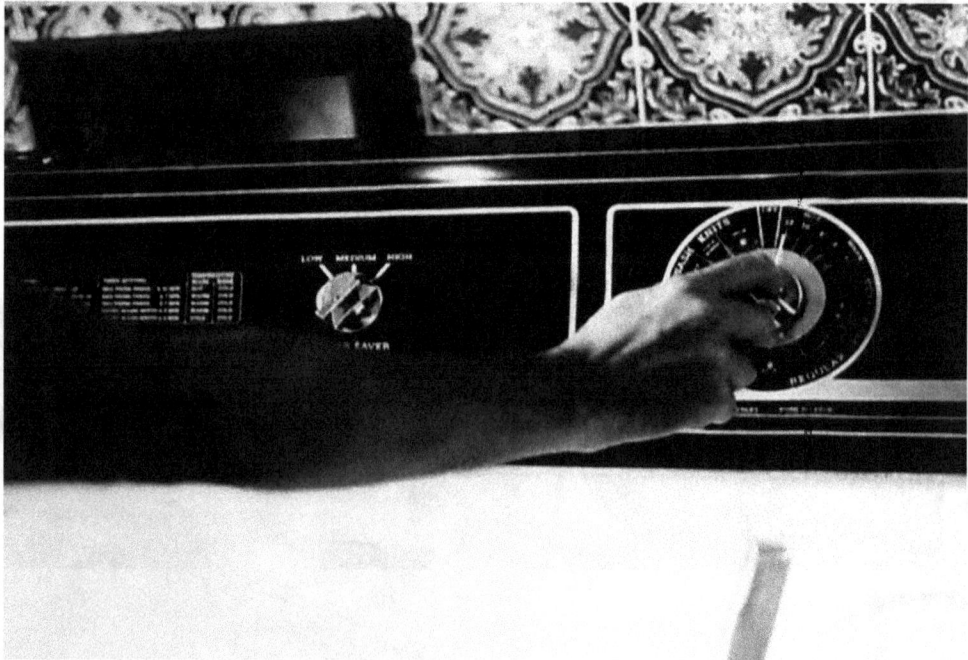

The recording I made of the zippers drying was ±45 minutes long. I submitted it to the "Cassette Mythos Audio Alchemy" CD/K7.

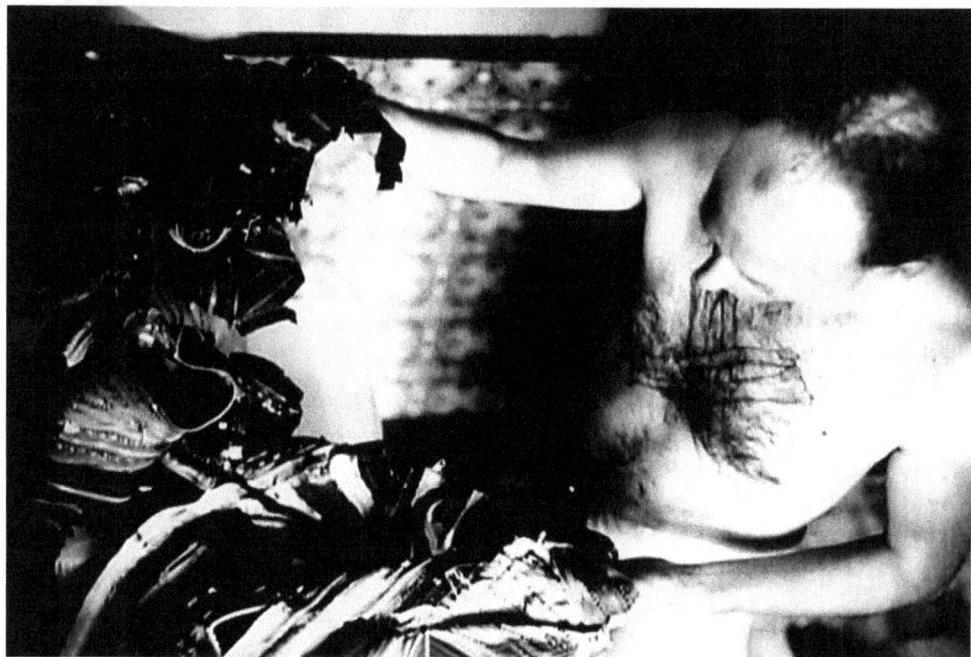

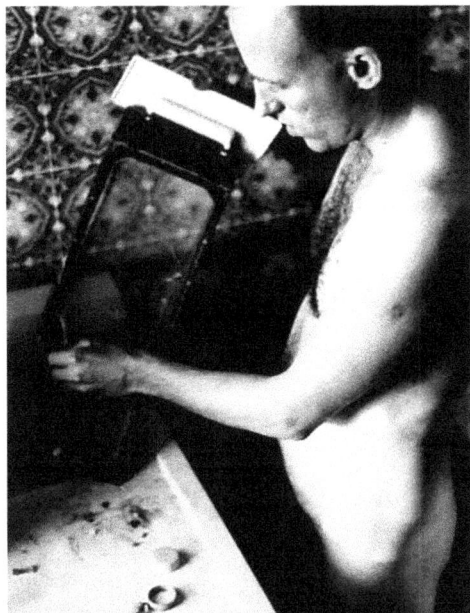

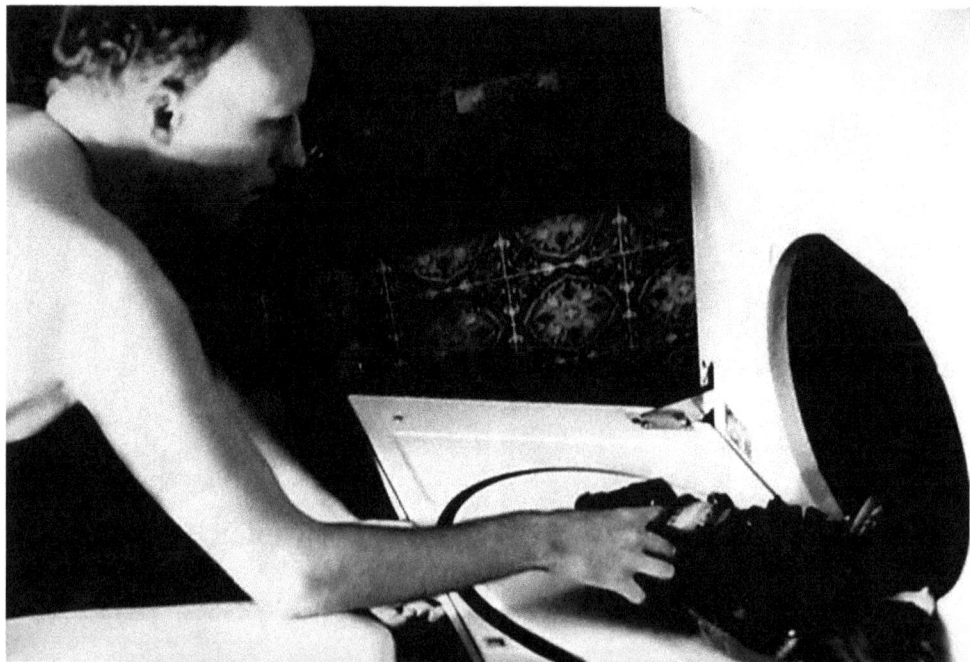

THE RESULT OF THE WASHING & DRYING WAS A TANGLED MESS THAT TOOK A LONG TIME TO DISENTANGLE SINCE THE ZIPPERS UNZIPPED & INTERPENETRATED..

THE CASSETTE MYTHOS AUDIO ALCHEMY CD/K7

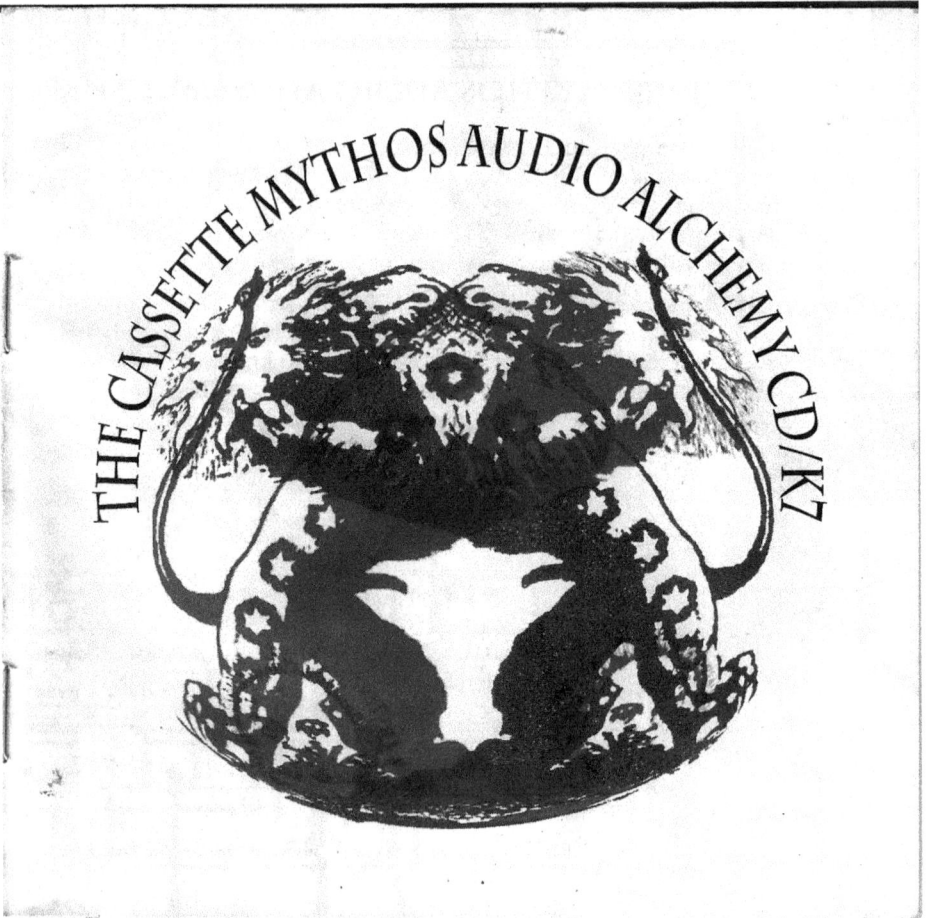

As I recall, contributors to the Audio Alchemy CD/K7 were asked to provide images that wd go w/ their section of the insert pamphlet. I provided one or more of the zipper wash'n'dry photos. In the final product, these weren't used. Instead, there was an overall design created by Sue Ann Harkey. I don't know whether that was b/c not enuf people submitted materials, or b/c not enuf submitted materials that the editors liked, or b/c it was just decided to go w/ an overall design look, or whatever. I was disappointed that none of my photos were used but I thought Harkey did a good design job so it was all good in the long run.

21. TENTATIVELY,
A CONVENIENCE
DRYING CLOTHES MADE ENTIRELY FROM ZIPPERS
(partial cycle)

wigemouth tapes
b. o. pox 382
cr(ater) bal
Trim
Ore
MD 21503
us@tgoth

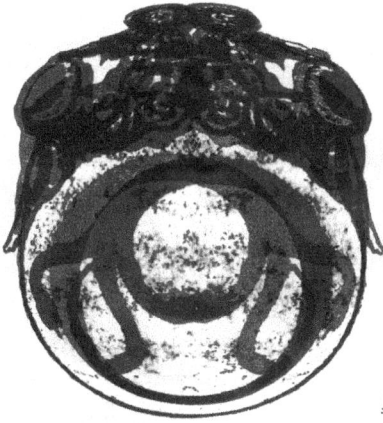

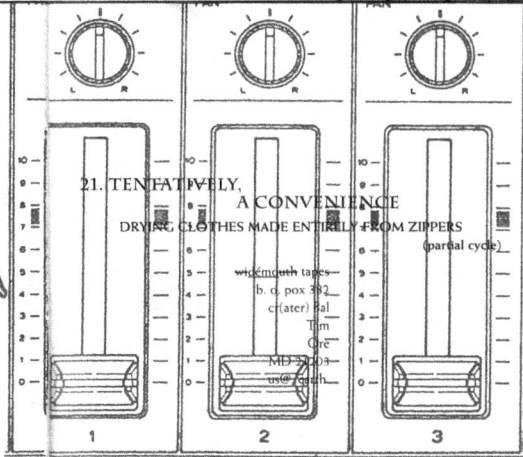

THE CASSETTE MYTHOS

AUDIO ALCHEMY CD/K7

AS IT TURNED OUT, THE EDITORS LIKED MY CONTRIBUTION SO MUCH THEY USED SOMETHING LIKE 16 MINUTES OF IT INSTEAD OF THE 21 SUGGESTED.

A DATE/TIME Dec. 8, 1991 E.V.	**B** DATE/TIME Dec. 8, 1991 E.V.
NOISE REDUCTION ☐ON ☐OFF	NOISE REDUCTION ☐ON ☐OFF

1, "CALEDONIA" - CROMAGNON - '69 - 3:42
" THE FEDERAL BUREAU OF NARCOTICS " - WILD MAN
2. FISCHER - '68 - 1:15
"THE MINOTAUR'S SONG " - THE INCREDIBLE
3. STRING BAND - '68 - 3:18
"DOG BREATH IN THE YEAR OF THE PLAGUE"
4. THE MOTHERS OF INVENTION - '68 - 5:31

5. "DIRTY OLD MAN" - THE FUGS - '66 - 2:49
CHARLES MANSON
6. "GARBAGE DUMP" - THE FAMILY - '68 - 2:32
"I WALK ON GILDED SPLINTERS" - DR. JOHN THE
7. NIGHT TRIPPER - '68 - 7:57

8. "JO LONER" - TIM BUCKLEY - '69 - 3:27

9. "OSCILLATIONS" - SILVER APPLES - ? - 2:49
"11 MUSTACHIOED DAUGHTERS" - BONZO DOG
10. BAND - '68 - 3:51
"SEVERAL SPECIES OF SMALL FURRY ANIMALS GATHERED
11. TOGETHER IN A CAVE & GROOVIN WITH A PICT - PINK FLOYD - TA-Ψ77
"PENA" - CAPTAIN BEEFHEART & HIS MAGIC BAND
12, - '69 - 2:31

• 1. "FANFARE - FIRE POEM" - ARTHUR BROWN - '68 - 1:54
• 2, "CROWN OF CREATION" - JEFFERSON AIRPLANE - '68 - 2:52
"SYMPATHY FOR THE DEVIL" - THE ROLLING STONES
• 3. - '68 - 6:14
"EVERYBODY'S GOT SOMETHING TO HIDE EXCEPT ME
• 4. AND MY MONKEY" - THE BEATLES - '68 - 2:25
• 5. "SUNSHINE OF YOUR LOVE" - CREAM - '67 - 4:08
"IF 6 WAS 9" - THE JIMI HENDRIX EXPERIENCE
• 6. - '67 - 5:33
• 7. "HOPE FOR HAPPINESS" - THE SOFT MACHINE - '68 - 4:20
• 8. "TWENTIETH CENTURY FOX" - THE DOORS - '67 - 2:30
"DON'T WORRY KYOKO - MUMMY'S ONLY LOOKING FOR
• 9. HER HAND IN THE SNOW" - YOKO ONO - '69 - 4:40
"GOOD TIMES BAD TIMES" - LED ZEPPELIN - '69 -
10. 2:43
• 11. "CRAWLING TO ETERNITY" - ALICE COOPER - '69 - 1:14
"THE BLACK ANGEL'S DEATH SONG" - THE VELVET
• 12. UNDERGROUND - '67 - 3:10
• 13. "MOTORCYCLE IRENE" - MOBY GRAPE - '68 - 2:16

⊕TDK 25 "POP" SONGS FROM '66 - '69 (E.V.) ▌SA90
THAT TENTATIVELY, A CONVENIENCE STILL LIKES
FOR CHRIS ASTIER

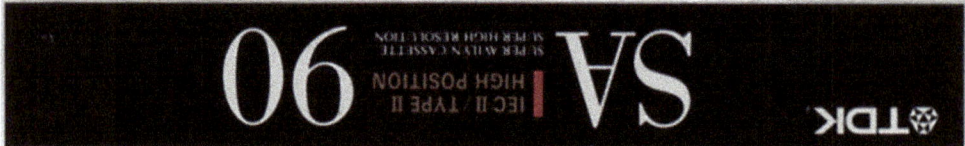

06 SA 90 TDK

IN 1992, I WAS LIVING IN A 4500 SQUARE FOOT WAREHOUSE
IN DOWNTOWN BALTIMORE. ONE OF MY ROOMMATES WAS CHRIS
ASTIER, AN EXCELLENT ELECTRIC BASS-PLAYER, POSSIBLY THE
BEST I'VE EVER PLAYED W/. HE WAS ONE OF THE 3 BASS-PLAYERS
IN MY "OFFICIAL" PROJECT, A BIG BAND W/ 17 MEMBERS AT ITS
PEAK, BUT USUALLY AN AVERAGE OF 12. FOR MOST OF THE
PEOPLE I'VE KNOWN THROUGHOUT MY LIFE, THE RESIDENTS
ARE THE EXEMPLAR OF WEIRDNESS, WHEREAS, TO ME, THEY'RE
POP MUSICIANS. I MUCH PREFER THE MUSIC OF JOHN CAGE,
MORTON FELDMAN, EARLE BROWN, CHRISTIAN WOLFF, IANNIS
XENAKIS, KARLHEINZ STOCKHAUSEN, FRANÇOIS BAYLE, PIERRE
HENRY, HARRY PARTCH, CONLON NANCARROW, ETC, ETC - WHOSE
WORK WD'VE BEEN FAR TOO 'WEIRD' FOR MOST OF MY FRIENDS IF
THEY EVEN EVER HEARD THEM ONCE. ANYWAY, CHRIS MUST'VE
ASKED ME FOR A MIX TAPE OF POP MUSIC I LIKE & I GAVE HIM THE
ABOVE.

ONE OF THE REASONS WHY THE RESIDENTS WERE COMMONLY
PERCEIVED AS THE HEIGHT OF WEIRDNESS WAS B/C MOST OF MY
MUSICIAN FRIENDS WERE IN BANDS THAT HAD SINGER-SONG-
WRITERS SO THEY WERE ACCUSTOMED TO THINKING IN THOSE
RATHER LIMITED TERMS & DIDN'T KNOW COMPOSERS.

1992.08.22

IT WAS VERY COMMON, ALMOST ALL-PREVAILING, FOR BANDS TO
HAVE PHOTOS OF THEMSELVES WEARING ALL BLACK & LOOKING
SULLEN & ANGRY. MAYBE THAT WAS SUPPOSED TO REFLECT
THEIR SOCIAL ENVIRONMENT BUT IT JUST SEEMED DUMB TO ME
- I WAS FROM THE EXTREMELY VIOLENT BalTimOre & I STILL HAD
THE SENSE OF HUMOR THAT THESE BANDS SEEMED TO LACK.

MARTHA COLBURN HAD LIVED W/ ME IN THE SAME WAREHOUSE
SPACE AS CHRIS BUT HAD MOVED UP A FLOOR. SHE GOT SOME
MICROFILM OF THE NATIONAL CANCER INSTITUTE THAT SHE
GAVE ME. THAT'S 16MM FILM W/O SPROCKETS SO I HAND-
PUNCHED SPROCKET-HOLES & MADE IT PROJECTABLE.

TALKATHON PROMOTION
BERLIN, APRIL 1, 1994E.V.
0:00- 3:05AM

IN 1994, I WAS FLOWN TO BERLIN, GERMANY, TO HELP BUILD &
RUN A TV STN INSTALLATION CALLED "TV HOSPITAL" IN THE
AKADEMIE DER KUNST IN WHAT HAD BEEN WEST BERLIN
(BERLIN WAS REUNITED AS OF 1989). THIS WAS A PROJECT OF
HERR STILETTO STUDIOS. THE ACTUAL TV STUDIO WAS IN THE
AKADEMIE NEXT TO THEIR CAFÉ & WE BROADCAST VERY LO-FI
OVER TELEPHONE LINES. THE ACTUAL INSTALLATION WAS MORE
COMPLEX THAN I'M WILLING TO GET INTO HERE BUT ONE PART OF
IT WAS A COUCH THAT WAS USED IN SOMEWHAT STANDARD TALK
SHOW FASHION AS A PLACE WHERE PEOPLE WOULD SIT & TALK.
WE HAD TO PROVIDE AS MUCH AS 15 HRS OF CONTENT A DAY FOR
THE OPEN TV CABLE CHANNEL WE WERE SENDING TO B/C THEIR
REGULAR PROGRAMMING WAS ONLY 9 HRS A DAY.

I PROPOSED A "TALKATHON", AN EVENT IN WCH COMPETITORS WD
TALK CONTINUOUSLY SIMULTANEOUSLY. THE 'WINNER' WD BE
THE LAST ONE TALKING. TO PROMOTE THIS, I TOLD A JOKE FOR
3 HRS ON APRIL 1ST. THE ABOVE IS A TITLE STILL FROM THE
MOVIE I MADE OF THAT PROMOTION.

1994.04.09

One way I used the couch was to turn it on its side, out of view of any (v)audience, then made the shot live & acted as if I were just sitting reading Thomas Pynchon's "Gravity's Rainbow". Then I threw the bk down as if I were done reading & the bk flew back into my lap.

1996.03.18

Sound Thinking - the Film(s)

- tentatively, a convenience
- March 18th, '96ev

I originally thought of "Sound Thinking" as that process in wch the reading of phonetic abbreviations/substitutions in text cd only be "understood" in their intended referentiality by imagining the sound & then translating it into the appropriate homonym (does this make me a homonymphomaniac? - or, perhaps, a homonymnphonemiac!). This was in the mid-'70s. The thing that fascinates me about this is that the reader must mentally "hear" the sounds (if not sounding them aloud) in order to "navigate" the labyrinth of the text. This is important because it's a hearing process that involves the memory of sound rather than sound itself! A deaf sighted person cdn't read such a text in the same way as a hearing sighted person (wch opens another area of interesting investigation). This brings to mind the, to me, somewhat odd expression: "I can't hear myself think!" - wch I've changed to: "A person who can't hear theirself think may not be a sound thinker."

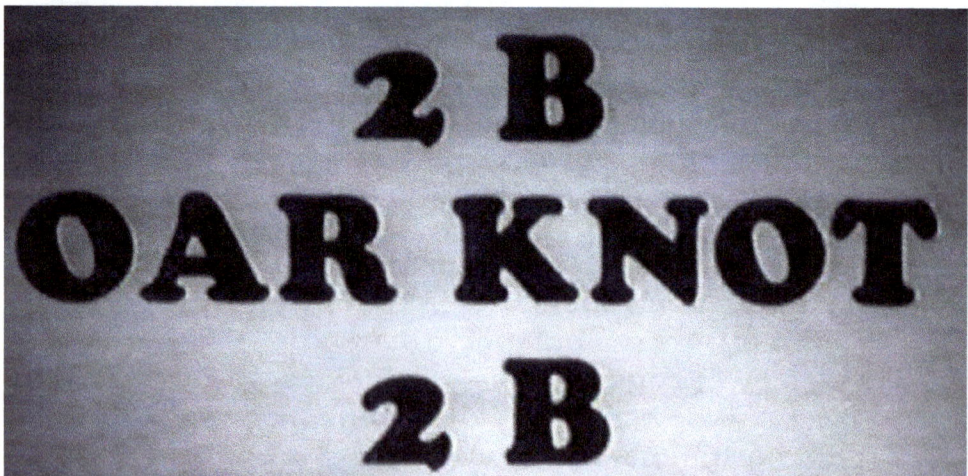

2 B
OAR KNOT
2 B

THE NEXT PHASE OF "SOUND THINKING" INVOLVED
PROGRAMMING A SYNTHESIZER (ORIGINALLY A DX7) &
SPEAKING THE TECHNICAL INFO ABOUT THIS PROGRAMMING
WHILE PROGRAMMING. THE "CONCLUSION" OF THIS BEING THAT
THE SOUND WD NOT BE PLAYED - IT'S EXISTENCE BEING LEFT IN
POTENTIA. THIS WAS IN MID-'86. SINCE I "KNEW" NEXT TO
NOTHING ABOUT PROGRAMMING SYNTHESIZERS AT THE TIME,
I DIDN'T "KNOW" WHETHER ANY SOUND WD BE PRODUCED BY
STRIKING A KEY (IN MANY INSTANCES OF EXPERIMENTATION
NONE WAS). ASSUMING THAT MOST MEMBERS OF THE
"AUD"IENCE WDN'T BE ABLE TO FOLLOW THE PROGRAMMING
INFO SUFFICIENTLY TO "KNOW" WHETHER ANY SOUND WD BE
PRODUCED EITHER, AT BEST, THE MOST PROBABLE WAY THAT
THIS "RIDDLE" CD BE SOLVED WD BE BY GETTING ACCESS TO THE
APPROPRIATE SYNTHESIZER, FOLLOWING THE PROGRAMMING
DIRECTIONS, & THEN "PLAYING" IT. THE IDEA BEING THAT THE
"AUD"IENCE WD GET THE INFO ABOUT HOW TO OSTENSIBLY
PRODUCE A PARTICULAR SOUND BUT WD HAVE TO GO THRU AN
UNLIKELY ORDEAL IN ORDER TO FIND OUT IF THE SOUND EVEN
"EXISTS". EVEN I WDN'T "KNOW" IF THE SOUND EXISTED. THIS
PUTS THE "SOUND" INTO A SORTOF "(IM)PROBABILITY LIMBO".

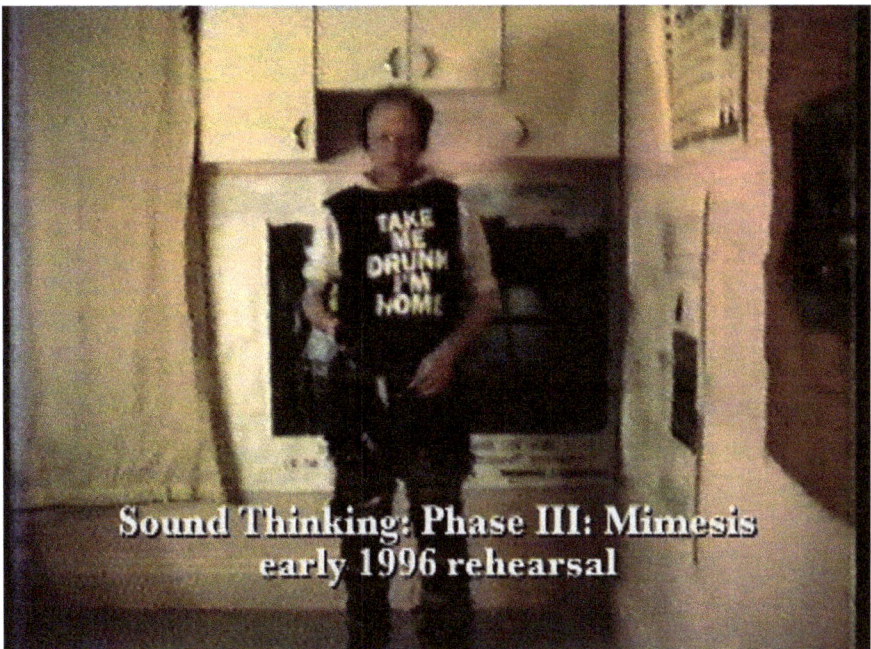

Sound Thinking: Phase III: Mimesis
early 1996 rehearsal

1996.03.18

THE 3RD PHASE OF "SOUND THINKING", CURRENTLY IN PROGRESS AS OF EARLY '96, INVOLVES, 1ST, THE PRE-RECORDING OF SOUNDS (IN THE 1ST VERSION MADE W/ FAIRLY CONVENTIONAL, USUALLY SMALL, INSTRUMENTS/"NOISE"-MAKERS). THESE SOUNDS ARE THEN PLAYED BACK, PREFERABLY W/ THE SOUND SYSTEM HIDDEN, WHILE SOMEONE MIMES THE PLAYING OF THESE SOUND-MAKERS. IN THIS CASE, THE VIEWING & HEARING "AUD"IENCE IS MOST LIKELY TO PERCEIVE THE INTENDED "MEANING" OF THE MIMING BY IDENTIFYING THE SOUNDS & THEN ASSOCIATING THEM W/ THEIR MEANS OF PRODUCTION. THIS MIGHT BE SAID TO GIVE A NEW MEANING TO THE TERM "STEREO SEPARATION" INSOFAR AS THAT BOTH THE SOUNDS & AN INCOMPLETE SET OF PHYSICAL ACTIONS USUALLY USED TO PRODUCE THOSE SOUNDS ARE PRESENT BUT SEPARATED FROM EACH OTHER BY VIRTUE OF THE ABSENCE OF THE "LINKING" INSTRUMENTS. THE IMAGINING OF THESE "MISSING LINKS" INVOLVES A SORTOF EMBRACING OF "SCHIZOPHONIA" WCH BECOMES "RESOLVED" IN THE PROCESS OF MENTALLY "PROJECTING" AN ABSENCE (THE INSTRUMENTS) INTO A "PRESENCE". BY SORTOF "ACCEPTING" AN ILLUSION AS AN IMPLIED PRESENCE, AN EXPLANATION OF THE MIMESIS IS PROVIDED.

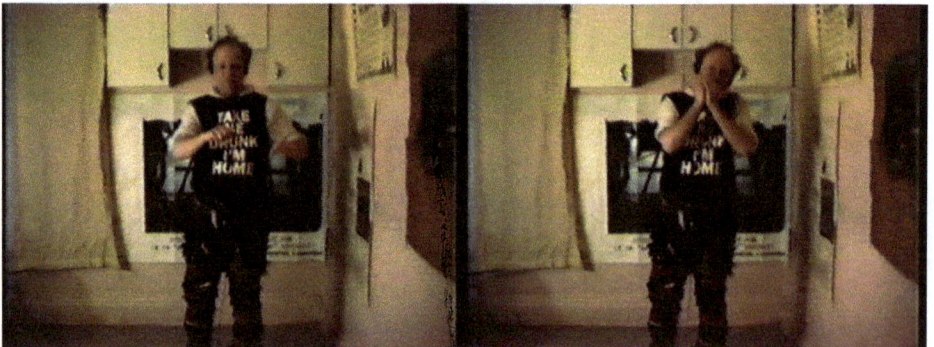

"Sound Thinking: Phase III: Mimesis" presented as a guerrilla action at the Ady statue in Budapest as part of a Neoist Festival on July 9, 1997.

"Sound Thinking: Phase III: Mimesis" presented along w/ a double projection of my films & vaudeo at Basement Films / Field & Frame in Abuquerque, New Mexico, us@ on Thursday, October 22, 1998.

THE MOST RECENT PHASE, ALSO CIRCA EARLY '96, INVOLVES ANOTHER SLIGHT DISPLACEMENT BETWEEN SIGHT & SOUND PECULIAR TO A PARTICULAR MEDIUM USUALLY ASSOCIATED W/ BOTH: FILM. THERE ARE 2 TYPES OF FILM SOUND MEDIUMS:

MAGNETIC STRIPING & OPTICAL STRIPING. IN THE FORMER (NO LONGER USED VERY OFTEN IN ANY SIZE OTHER THAN SUPER-8MM), A STRIP OF TAPE IS ENCODED W/ AN ELECTRO-MAGNETIC SIGNAL WCH, WHEN DECODED THRU THE CORRESPONDING PLAYBACK MACHINERY, PRODUCES THE SOUND. IN THE LATTER, A PATTERN OF LIGHT IS USED AS THE ENCODING INSTEAD. OF THESE, THERE ARE 2 TYPES: VARIABLE DENSITY & VARIABLE AREA. THE FORMER IS SIMPLY A PATTERN OF PARALLEL LINES OF DIFFERING WIDTHS, THE LATTER BEING A MORE "BIOMORPHIC" CORRELATIVE TO THE SOUND (OF GREATER FIDELITY).

IN THE CURRENT TECHNICAL CONFIGURATION, THE SOUND ENCODING IS PARALLEL & ADJACENT TO THE VISUALS - BUT THE VISUALS CAN BE SEEN AS IMAGES WITHOUT ANY INTERVENING "TRANSLATION" EQUIPMENT (ALTHOUGH, OBVIOUSLY, PROJECTION IS USUALLY USED). THE SOUND ENCODING, HOWEVER, IS ONLY AUDIBLE AS SOUND THRU THE MEDIUM OF MACHINERY PLAYBACK. THRU A SIMPLE DISPLACEMENT OF THE SOUND ENCODING (IN THIS CASE, OPTICAL STRIPING) FROM ITS ORDINARY FILMIC POSITION TO ITS ADJACENT POSITION IN THE VISUALS FRAMING FIELD, THE ENCODED INFO IS PRESENTED - BUT W/O ITS ORDINARY DECODING.

FURTHERMORE, IT'S IMPORTANT TO TAKE INTO CONSIDERATION THAT SOUND IS CONTINUOUS IN FILM BUT VISUALS ARE DISCONTINUOUSLY PRESENTED AS A SEQUENCE OF STILLS AT A CERTAIN AMOUNT OF FRAMES PER SECOND (USUALLY 16 TO 24). BECAUSE OF THIS, THE DISPLACEMENT OF THE SOUND INFO, WHILE PRESENTED ALMOST IN ITS ENTIRETY (MINUS A BIT OF FRAME-LINE INTERRUPTION), CAUSES THE SOUND INFO TO BE PERCEIVABLE IN A WAY NOT NATURAL TO SOUND. I.E.: AS BYTES THAT CAN BE ANAYLYZED, ON A FRAME-BY-FRAME LEVEL, INDEPENDENT OF THEIR USUAL LINEAR CONFIGURATION IN TIME - I.E.: THRU VISUAL CORRELATION THEY CAN BE PERCEIVED IN WAYS PECULIAR TO VISUAL PHENOMENA.

1996.03.18

THE IMPLICATION BEING THAT THE CREATION OF CORRELATIVES
PERCEIVABLE THRU DIFFERENT SENSES THAN THAT USED TO
PERCEIVE THE ORIGINAL STIMULI ENABLES ONE TO RETHINK
THAT STIMULI FROM ANGLES THAT CD BE SAID TO BE
SIMULTANEOUSLY "IMAGINARY" (AS "UN-NATURAL" PROPERTIES
OF THE ORIGINAL STIMULI - SUCH AS, IN THE CASE UNDER STUDY,
THE LINEAR TIME "FREEZING" MENTIONED ABOVE, THE STILL
FRAMING, & SUPERIMPOSITION FROM PERSISTENCE OF VISION)
& AS "REAL" (AS ULTIMATELY PRODUCTIVE OF THE "NATURAL"
QUALITIES OF THE STIMULUS WHEN PLAYED BACK THRU THE
APPROPRIATE APPARATUS).

PICTOGRAMETING

- The sidewalks of downtown Pittsburgh, us⊗
- Saturday, November 30th, 1996, 1:30 to 3:30PM

photos: Fabio Roberti & Donna Blicharz

tENTATIVELY, a cONVENIENCE

1996.11.30

I made a 32 X 40 inch picket sign with graphics on both sides & no words. On 1 side I painted in red highly bit-mapped images of, "reading" from left to right & top to bottom, a pair of scissors ($)"chasing" an airplane (() overtop a mathematical symbol of 3 horizontal lines with a diagonal slash thru them (something like this: ≠) next to a check mark in a rectangular box (something like this: [√)]. The pixilation of these symbols rendered them almost incomprehensible as any of the above. This was partially "remedied" by drawing over them with black marker. On the other side was a drawing using black marker again of the international pictograms for telegrams & bathtubs. The image for telegrams shows a lightning bolt across a card. This was placed so that the bolt is headed into the tub. These symbols were largely chosen as "nonsense" although the lightning/tub-with-water juxtaposition was calculated to be provocative/ evocative. Since this picket was made with the intention of using it in "guerrilla" actions, I researched the Pennsylvania laws regarding picketing, etc, to try to learn about what I could be arrested for. The only remotely relevant law I found was:

from:
Purdon's Pennsylvania Statutes
and Pennsylvania Consolidated Statutes Annotated

Statute 5507. Obstructing highways and other public passages

   (a) Obstructing. - A person, who, having no legal privilege to do so, intentionally or recklessly obstructs any highway, railroad track or public utility right-of-way, sidewalk, navigable waters, other public passage, whether alone or with others, commits a summary offense, or, in case he persists after warning by a law officer, a misdemeanor of the third degree. No person shall be deemed guilty of an offense under this subsection solely because of a gathering of persons to hear him speak or otherwise communicate, or solely because of being a member of such a gathering.

   (b) Refusal to move on. -
        (1) A person in a gathering commits a summary offense if he refuses to obey a reasonable official request or order to move:
             (i) to prevent obstruction of a highway or other public passage; or
             (ii) to maintain public safety by dispersing those gathered in dangerous proximity to a fire or other hazard.
        (2) An order to move, addressed to a person whose speech or other lawful behavior attracts an obstructing audience, shall not be deemed reasonable if the obstruction can be readily remedied by police control of the size or location of the gathering.

   (c) Definition. - As used in this section the word "obstructs" means renders impassable without unreasonable inconvenience or hazard.

Underlining mine. - anonymous

One of the things that I found interesting about this was the use of the word "reasonable". It's funny to me, e.g., that if "obstructs" is defined as "without unreasonable hazard" it's considered "reasonable"to arrest someone for it. As usual, I wonder about how valid I would find any arbiter of "reasonable" to be in a courtroom situation. This law text was then printed out in "Zapf Dingbats 1" font to encode it & make it unreadable as any sort of "straight" statement. Fifty copies of this were printed in black on red card-stock.

The street action consisted of my "picketing" with the sign & giving people the hand-out as an "explanation" when they were extroverted &/or friendly enough to approach me. The basic intent was to use the "loaded" context of the picket sign to try to catalyze people into reading a "heavy" meaning into what might otherwise ordinarily be hardly even noticed as "just a picture" or as "nonsense". I got into at least 30 fairly interesting interactions with people during this. One young girl thought it meant that " people should stop drownding their children". An adult with her explained to me that there had been alot about that on the news lately. When people asked me what it meant I gave various responses. Sometimes I said "The beginning is near!" as a variation on the old "The end is near!" cliché. Sometimes I told people it meant "nothing" & that "I just like to walk around with this & see how people react." Sometimes I asked people to interpret it for me.

photo: Greg Pierce

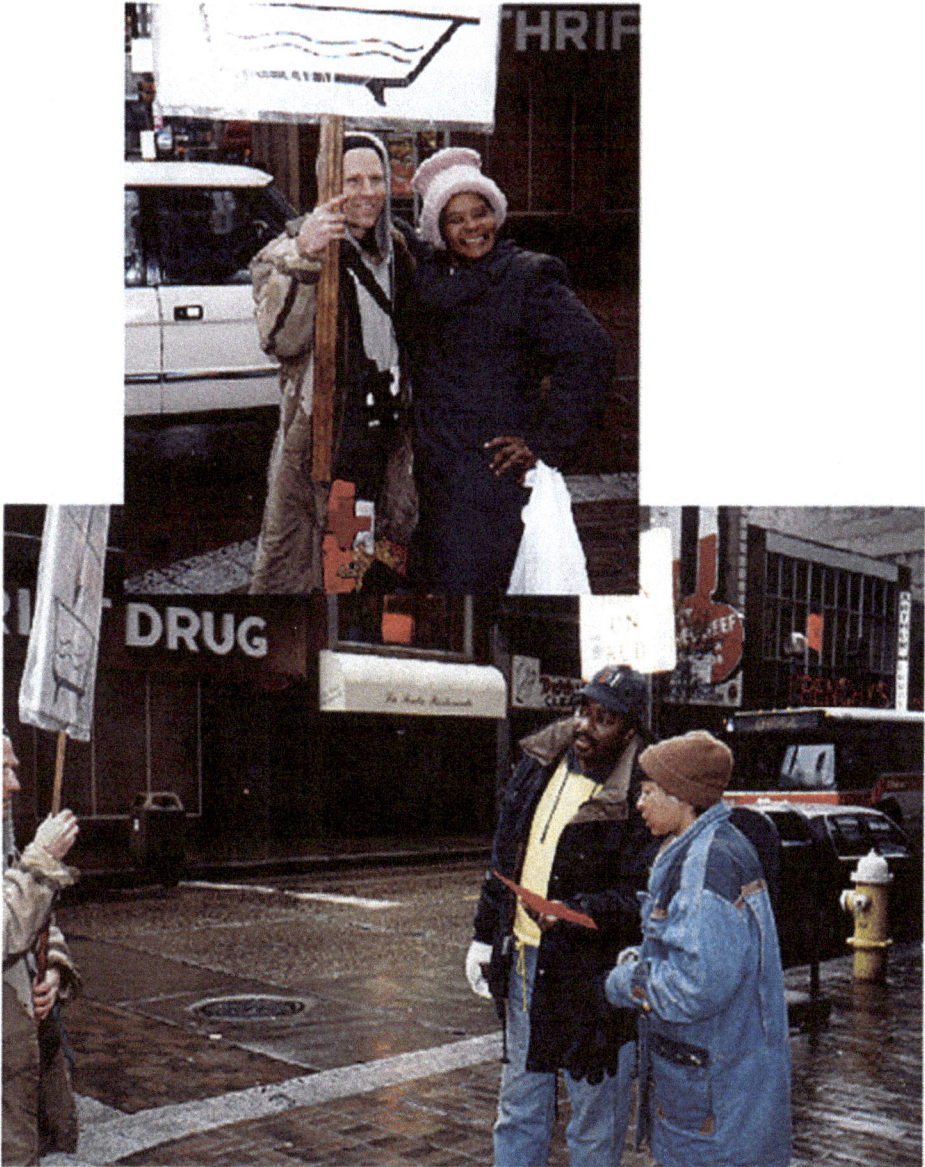

Four friends of mine (Fabio & Donna & Alisa & Greg) followed me at a discrete distance & photographed me. One drunk guy noticed that he was being photoed & aggressively confronted them wanting to know why he was being photographed & whether "he'd passed the test."

1996.11.30

One guy interpreted the telegrams/bathtubs sign as meaning "de-oppression" (or some such). He claimed to've once been on death row & said that it made him think of that & electrocution.

One of these 2 guys speculated that the scissors "chasing" the airplane might be trying to "clip its wings." I particularly liked that explanation.

Sometimes when I gave out the hand-out as a "souvenir" I explained that if people typed it into their computers in "Zapf Dingbats" font & then converted it into a text font they'd "get a punchline". One of these people even seemed remotely likely to try it.

1996.11.30

MISSION! in SPACE!

FREE AD to RAVE

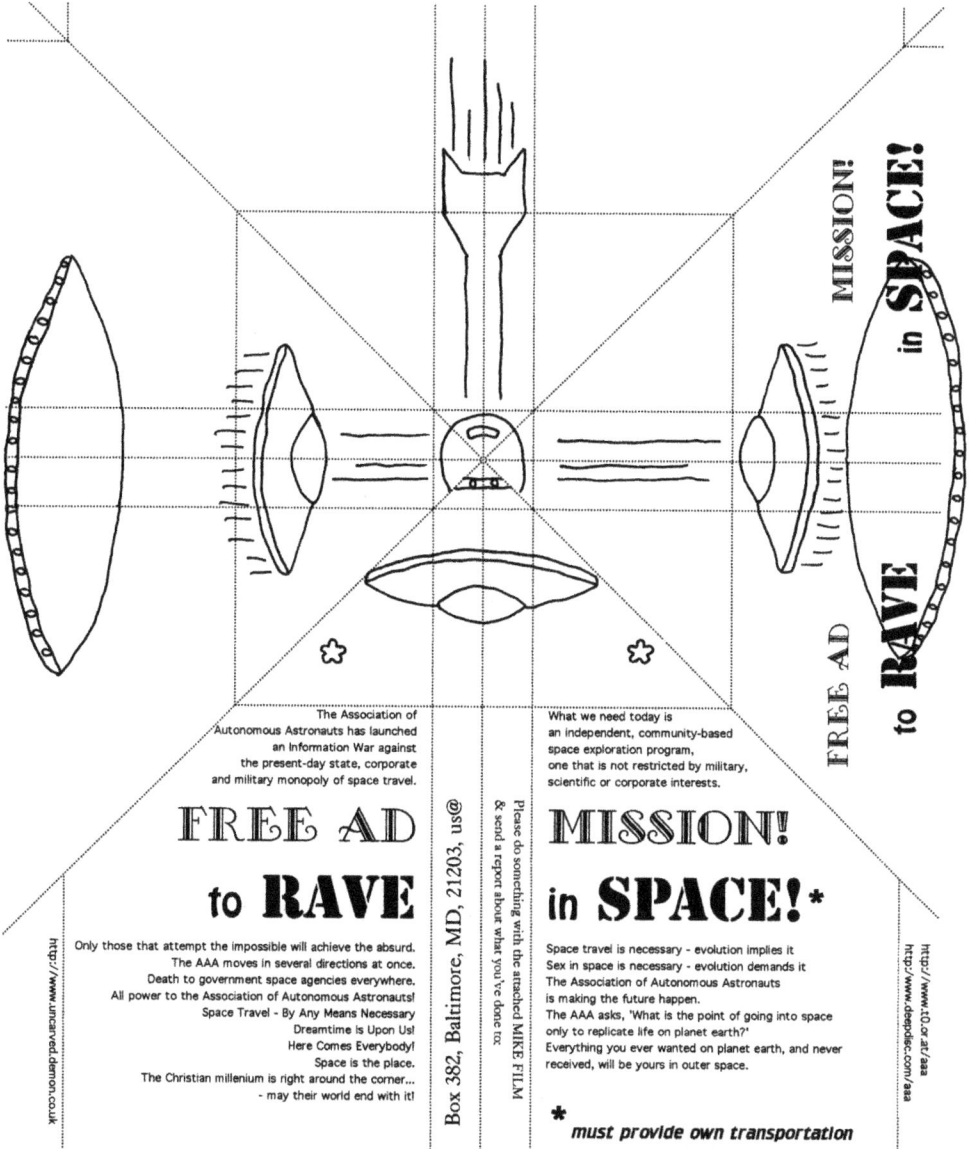

The Association of Autonomous Astronauts has launched an Information War against the present-day state, corporate and military monopoly of space travel.

What we need today is an independent, community-based space exploration program, one that is not restricted by military, scientific or corporate interests.

FREE AD to RAVE

MISSION! in SPACE!*

Only those that attempt the impossible will achieve the absurd.
The AAA moves in several directions at once.
Death to government space agencies everywhere.
All power to the Association of Autonomous Astronauts!
Space Travel - By Any Means Necessary
Dreamtime Is Upon Us!
Here Comes Everybody!
Space is the place.
The Christian millenium is right around the corner...
- may their world end with it!

Space travel is necessary - evolution implies it
Sex in space is necessary - evolution demands it
The Association of Autonomous Astronauts
is making the future happen.
The AAA asks, 'What is the point of going into space
only to replicate life on planet earth?'
Everything you ever wanted on planet earth, and never
received, will be yours in outer space.

* must provide own transportation

Please do something with the attached MIKE FILM
& send a report about what you've done to:

Box 382, Baltimore, MD, 21203, us@

http://www.uncarved.demon.co.uk

http://www.t0.or.at/aaa
http://www.deepdisc.com/aaa

ON MY BIRTHDAYS IN 1997 & IN 1998 I FLEW OVER BALTIMORE (1997) & PITTSBURGH (1998) IN A SMALL PLANE PILOTED BY DS BAKKER & THREW OUT SLIGHTLY LESS THAN 1,000 PAPER AIRPLANES OF THE TYPE THAT FLIES IN LOOP-DE-LOOPS. IT WAS A GREAT JOY TO SEE THEIR AEROBATICS AT ROUGHLY 100MPH. THE ABOVE IS WHAT WAS PRINTED ON THE 2ND OF THE AIR DROP PLANES. THEY WERE DESIGNED TO PRODUCE A CRUDE ANIMATION WHEN THEY WERE UNFOLDED.

The Association of
Autonomous Astronauts has launched
an Information War against
the present-day state, corporate
and military monopoly of space travel.

FREE AD

to RAVE

Only those that attempt the impossible will achieve the absurd.

The AAA moves in several directions at once.

Death to government space agencies everywhere.

All power to the Association of Autonomous Astronauts!

Space Travel - By Any Means Necessary

Dreamtime Is Upon Us!

Here Comes Everybody!

Space is the place.

The Christian millenium is right around the corner...

- may their world end with it!

Box 382, Baltimore, MD, 21203, us@

Please do something with the attached MIKE FILM
& send a report about what you've done to:

What we need today is
an independent, community-based
space exploration program,
one that is not restricted by military,
scientific or corporate interests.

MISSION!

in SPACE!*

Space travel is necessary - evolution implies it

Sex in space is necessary - evolution demands it

The Association of Autonomous Astronauts
is making the future happen.

The AAA asks, 'What is the point of going into space
only to replicate life on planet earth?'

Everything you ever wanted on planet earth, and never
received, will be yours in outer space.

*

must provide own transportation

NOTE THE PIECE OF MIKE FILM ATTACHED.

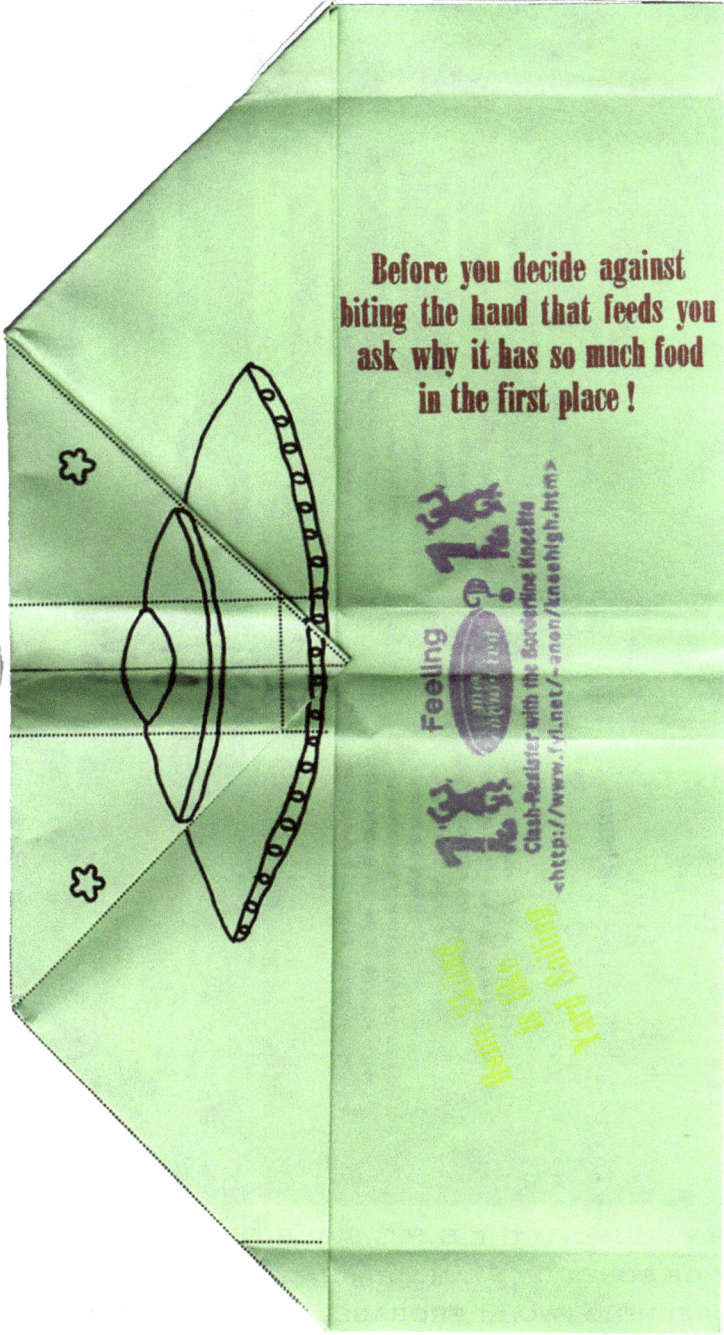

Before you decide against
biting the hand that feeds you
ask why it has so much food
in the first place !

Feeling

Cash-Register with the Borderline Knectie
<http://www.fyi.net/~anon/kneehigh.htm>

Never Skimp
Is like
Yard Sailing

1998.09

I PROBABLY FOUNDED THE S.P.C.S.M.E.F. IN 1997 OR 1998 AS
A PARODY OF SORTS OF STAN BRAKHAGE AFTER I WITNESSED HIM
GIVE A SCREENING (WCH I PROBABLY PROJECTED) & A TALK. I
FOUND HIM TO BE ASTOUNDINGLY POMPOUS. HE EXPLAINED THAT
HE FILMED SEA MONKEYS TO PRODUCE A HYPNOGOGIC EFFECT.

HENCE, S.P.C.S.M.E.F. = SOCIETY FOR THE PREVENTION OF CRUELTY TO SEA MONKEYS BY EXPERIMENTAL FILMMAKERS. I'D GOTTEN A WHALE PLUSHY (WCH I LATER LEARNED WAS "SHAMU") & REMOVED ITS STUFFING & OTHERWISE MODIFIED IT SO I CD WEAR IT.

THE IDEA WAS THAT I'D LOOK LIKE I WAS BEING EATEN BY A BIG
FISH (UNCONVINCINGLY) & SHAT OUT THE OTHER END.

THE CONVERTED PLUSHY BECAME MY OUTFIT TO WEAR WHEN
GIVING SPCSMEF PRESENTATIONS. THE PHOTOS WERE
PROBABLY TAKEN BY FABIO ROBERTI BUT MAY'VE BEEN TAKEN
BY ETTA CETERA, MY PARTNER IN GRIME. THIS WAS FROM MY
1ST TRIP TO CONEY ISLAMD (IT WAS CLOSED).

PITTSBURGH CITY PAPER, NOV 15 - NOV 22, 2000

LOCAL VOCALS

A conversation with tENTATIVELY, a cONVENIENCE

Interviewer: JO REICHENBACHER

Photographer: HEATHER MULL

By day, tENTATIVELY, a cONVENIENCE is a mild-mannered projectionist and exhibit technician in cultural institutions such as The Andy Warhol Museum. But tINY has numerous other projects from which he rarely, if ever, profits financially — projects intended to disrupt the ordinary way people think.

How did your name come to be tENTATIVELY, a cONVENIENCE?

It is the answer to the question "What is a name?" It is tentatively a convenience.

Tell me about your tattoos.

I have a good number of splotch tattoos that are relevant to me being the president and founder of the National Association for the Advancement of Multi-Colored Peoples (NAAMCP). I have a splotch on my hand, my back, my arm, a couple on my leg and a splotch on my eyebrow. My splotch tattoos represent a gradual changing of skin color. I like the idea of having multi-colored skin because I think the obsession of this society with so-called race is a pain in the ass.

What other tattoos do you have?

On my leg I have a glow-in-the-dark tattoo of a dust mite enlarged 250 times which looks like a fine scar in normal lighting, but once charged and glowing in the dark is quite visible. The idea is that dust mites live off of dead human skin. So people pay to me. "Doesn't that glow-in-the-dark ink cause your skin to die?" I like the idea of an image of something causing a situation that feeds what the image is of. It's an ecological joke.

You have referred to yourself as a "sprocket scientist." What exactly is that?

In 1978, I made the transition from artist to mad scientist. I took the 20 art objects I had made at the time and shot 13 50-foot Super 8 films of them

and then gave away the art objects. I then cut the film into individual frames, totaling 46,800 frames of film and started to distribute those frames of film around the world, which I have been doing now for 22 years. By cutting the films and distributing them individually, it forces the creation of a situation where the audience is not going to perceive the film in any ordinary way.

One friend of mine went to Russia, to a prostitute's house that he thought was probably a KGB agent trying to get information out of him. He left the frames of film scattered around the apartment in the hopes that the KGB would pick up the film and try to figure what the fuck they were all about. That's pretty much what sprocket science is all about. Finding ways to use ordinary mass media to get people our of their ordinary states of mind. I would like to help create a society in which people can live by their imagination, in which people are thoughtful and in which people are happy.

Does anyone ever think you are insane?

In most societies, the idea of criminally insane is accepted because being a criminal is considered to be bad and being insane is considered to be bad, so those words fit together comfortably in most people's minds.

I pose the idea of being criminally sane: People willing to

break laws in order to support their own moral system. It would be criminally sane, for example, if you were poor and had you no place to live, to squat a house. It might be illegal, but it's criminally sane. It's more sane than accepting that you have to live outside because you don't have the money to pay someone that doesn't, in my opinion, deserve it in the first place.

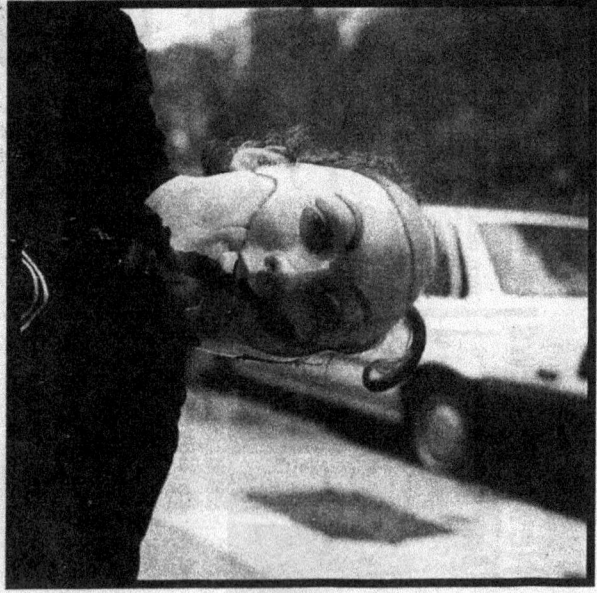

ONE OF MY FAVORITE THINGS TO DO IS TO STAGE PHOTOGRAPHS FOR NEWSPAPER ARTICLES ABOUT ME. IT SEEMS THAT WHAT MOST PEOPLE DO, AT BEST, IS JUST STAND THERE WHILE THE PRESS PHOTOGRAPHER SNAPS THEM. I PREFER TO GO THAT EXTRA MILE. AS W/ MANY THINGS I CREATE, I HOPE TO GENERATE A DOUBLE-TAKE IN THE VIEWER.

IN MY CAPACITY AS THE PROJECTIONIST AT THE ANDY WARHOL MUSEUM IN PITTSBURGH (WHERE I WORKED FOR 20 YRS) I PROJECTED "LIGHT SHOWS (SORTOF)" FOR BANDS THAT PLAYED IN THE THEATER. I HAD FUN DOING THIS & PUT IN SUBSTANTIAL EFFORT DESPITE THE PATHETICALLY LOW PAY & ZERO ACKNOWLEDGEMENT OF MY CREATIVITY.

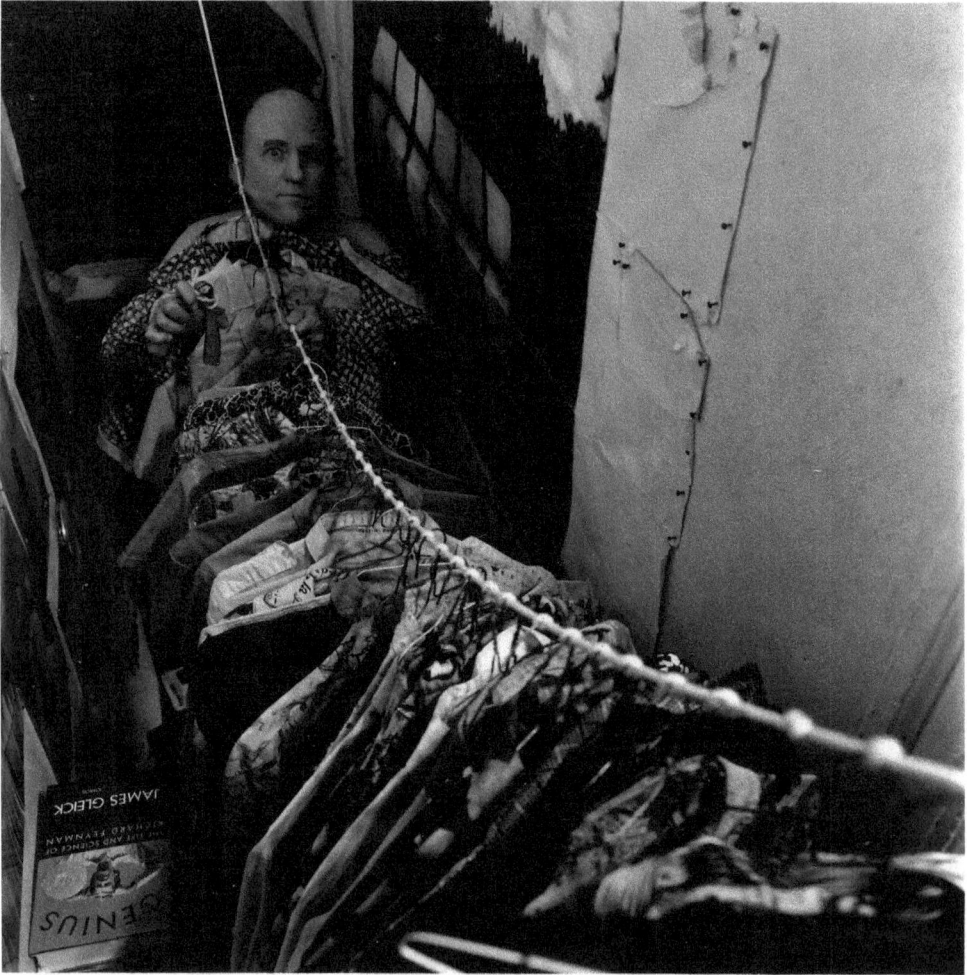

IN JANUARY, 2005, JULIE GONZALEZ MOVED TO PITTSBURGH
WHERE WE MET AT AN ANTI-WAR PROTEST HELD IN EXTREMELY
COLD WEATHER. WE QUICKLY BONDED AS EX-BALTIMOREANS,
ANARCHISTS, & PHOTOGRAPHY ENTHUSIASTS. I WAS LIVING IN
A SMALL HOUSE WHERE I HAD HUNG A CLOTHESLINE OVER THE
THE STAIRWELL FROM THE 1ST FLOOR TO THE 2ND FLOOR &
HUNG MANY OF MY CLOTHES ON IT. IT WAS AWKWARD & HEAVY
TO HAUL UP & DOWN BUT IT MADE A GOOD PHOTO PROP.

JULIE & I WENT FOR A WALK WHERE WE SHOT PHOTOS
RELEVANT TO MY RECENT MATH TATTOO I CALL MY "PARADIGM
SHIFT KNUCKLE SANDWICH"". I'M SHOWN ENGRAVING ITS
FORMULA IN THE GROUND IN THE TOP PHOTO & THEN A SCAN
OF THE TATTOO ON MY KNUCKLES IS PHOTOGRAPHED ON THE
TRACKS IN THE BOTTOM IMAGE.

FROM THE SAME SHOOT: THE SHADOW-PLAY EXTENDS THE
INFINITY SYMBOL ON MY LEFT MIDDLE FINGER.

PITTSBURGH CITY PAPER ~ OCT 4-11, 2006

▶FILM

Know Return

[BY BILL O'DRISCOLL]
DRISCOLL@STEELCITYMEDIA.COM

TO BE UNDERSTOOD is a luxury. According to tENTATIVELY, a CONVENIENCE, it can also be boring. As a filmmaker, writer, performer and multipurpose provocateur, his goal is to give audiences new experiences — even if that means they won't know what the hell is going on. At the Oct. 10 installment of the Film Kitchen screening series, Tent will show video to complement readings from his new book, *Footnotes.*

One video, "B.T.O.U.C.," documents a performance that got him arrested: a 1983 New Year's Eve party in a Baltimore sewer tunnel that involved nudity, two dog carcasses and accusations that Tent was a cult leader — even though, as he notes, at the time he was so unpopular that he "couldn't find a roommate."

HOW IS IT NOT UNDERSTANDING FRUITFUL?

That's an obsession of mine, because one common performer philosophy is that one should be populist. One should have a clear agenda, a clear message, and one should get across that message in a way that reaches the most people. But my attitude is that people tend to be too simple-minded, and that it's good to challenge people's simple-mindedness with what I call "conceptual obstacle courses."

What I sometimes try to do is create a situation that I'm fairly sure will not be easily understood with ideas based on people's previous ideas or their prejudices, in the hope that it will stimulate them to think in a new way, or, let's say, create new neural pathways in their brain.

DO PEOPLE RESPOND AS YOU'D HOPE?

What more typically happens is that people just superimpose wildly inappropriate stereotype projections on the situation, instead of learning something new from it.

YOUR ESSAY "REACTIONARY MUDDLE AMERICA" CENTERS ON STUDENTS' WRITTEN REACTIONS TO A 1992 PERFORMANCE AND VIDEO PRESENTATION AT THE UNIVERSITY OF MARYLAND.

As is evident by reading those papers, the students just couldn't handle it and had a very reactionary reaction to it, "reactionary" meaning in this case "close-minded" — but shockingly so, to me.

What the students did was generally pick one pretty small aspect of the performance and blow it out of proportion to an extreme extent. They generally disliked that I used sexual footage. But the sexual footage constituted an extreme minority of the evening. For example, I used a loop of a penis starting to enter a vagina and then popping back out again. And it was meant to be a tension-building device — something that would keep them on the edge of their seats, because obviously people would have this biological need for the penis to finally succeed in penetrating, but it never does. And it was driving them crazy. I knew it would! But it was also an extremely minor aspect of what was going on.

THE SHOW ALSO INCLUDED VIDEO OF THE ONE WORD PER PERSON PARTY.

I have been to many, many parties over the years, and I found most of little imagination to them. So some friends and I tried to throw different types of parties, like nudist parties, or whatever. Once there was the One Word Per Person Party, where we all decided to restrict ourselves to just one word for two hours, and say that word over and over

again. The interesting part was to see which word each person would pick. One person picked the word "kiss," and she only said it when she was kissing people. Another person picked the word "random," and he only said it when the second hand of his watch reached 12 — so he never said it at a random time. Another person said "Ialochezia," which means the use of vulgar language for the release of tension. It became interesting to see how expressive you could be with your one word.

WHAT DID THE STUDENTS THINK?

The students utterly, utterly hated it, and just thought we were morons for doing something like this. And yet I think if you were to go to the average party, if there is such a thing, you'd find that the conversations are often conceptually repetitive in a way that's not really so far off from people saying one word.

Not a single [student] really addressed what the movie what actually about. One student described the One Word Per Person Party as "the party where everybody just says dirty words." In the book I psychoanalyze why he did this in a way that is definitely not flattering to him.

WHY RESPOND TO THE STUDENTS' COMMENTS AT ALL?

It's a source of frustration to me when the opportunity to have one's mind challenged and consciousness expanded is responded to with the opposite effect — with the contraction of thinking. I respond to those papers because I wanted to refute their contraction, and I wanted to refute it in great detail in order to demonstrate that I am very serious about what I am doing, and I am thinking about it, and it's not just random noise, which is what people often

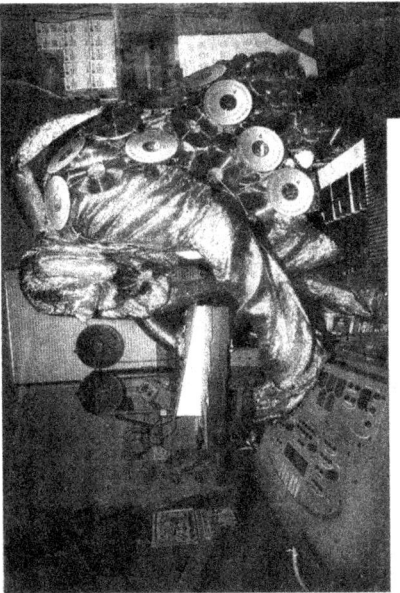
PHOTO: HEATHER MULL
Tent at work: tENTATIVELY, a CONVENIENCE in his studio.

FILM KITCHEN
8 p.m. Tue. Oct. 10
(7 p.m. reception).
Melwood. $4.
412-316-3342, x178

HERE'S YET-ANOTHER INSTANCE WHERE I GOT TO SIGNIFICANTLY EXPAND THE 'SUBJECT PORTRAIT' BEYOND ITS USUAL PARAMETERS.

FOR 18 YRS NOW, JULIE GONZALEZ HAS BEEN MAKING HERSELF
AVAILABLE FOR HELPING ME W/ MY PROJECTS REGARDLESS OF
HOW BUSY SHE IS. IN THIS CASE, SHE SHAVED THIS SYMBOL
INTO MY HAIR (IN HER ROLE AS "CIVILIAN BARBER") & THEN
PHOTOGRAPHED IT. IT'S A BLISSYMBOL MEANING "OPEN" SO
I THINK OF IT COMBINED W/ MY 3D BRAIN TATTOO AS "OPEN MIND".

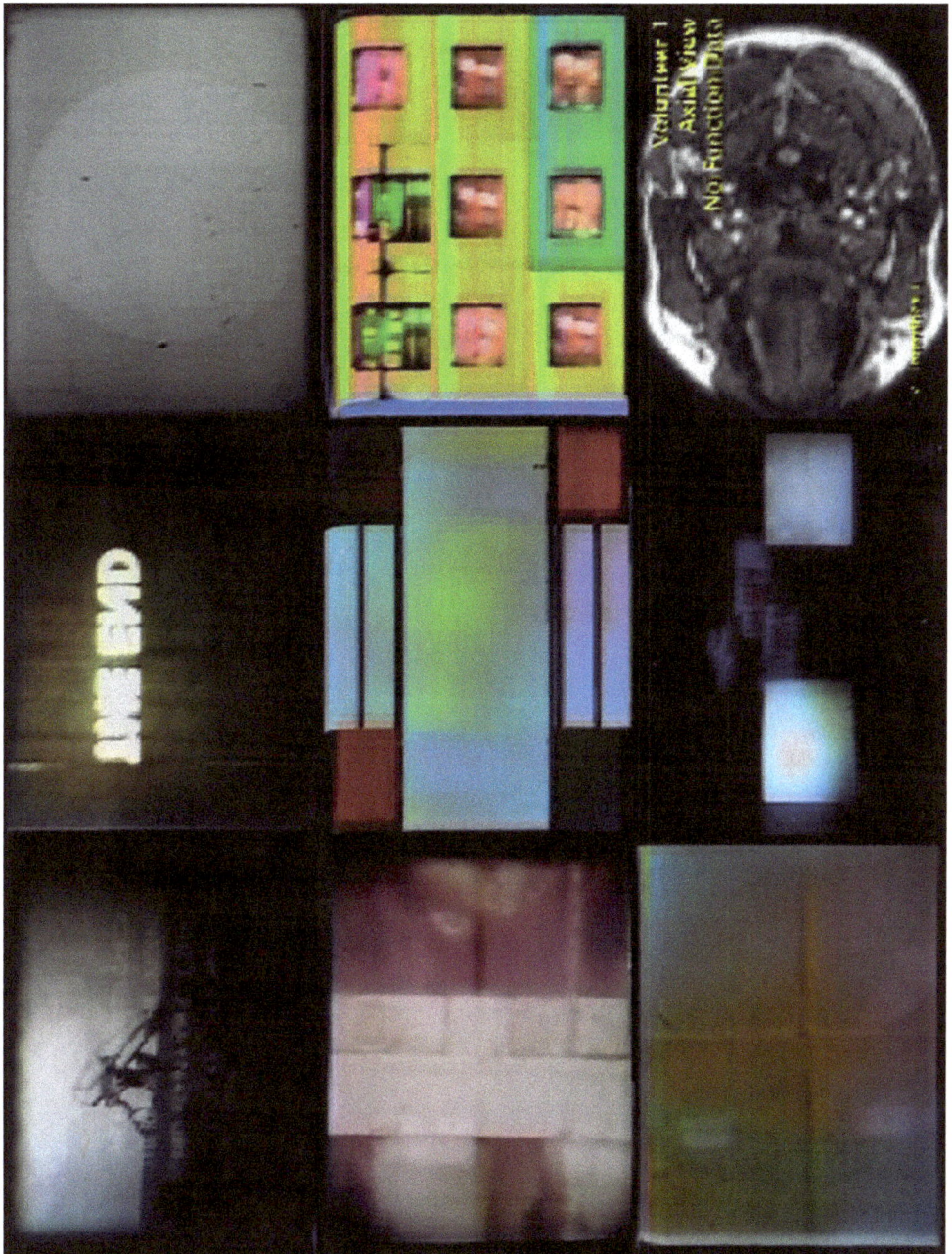

I'VE BEEN MAKING A SERIES OF MOVIES SINCE 1980 CALLED "SUBTITLES". THIS IS FROM THE "(9 IMAGES VERSION)". FOR IT, I TOOK THE 9 EARLIER VERSIONS & EDITED THEM ALL SO THAT THEY WERE IN SYNC W/ EACH OTHER & THEN PUT THEM ALL W/IN THE SAME FRAME. THIS IS ONE STILL FROM THAT VERSION.

IN 2008, ARTIST ALLY REEVES CURATED A SORT OF 'CABINET OF CURIOSITIES" AT THE CHILDREN'S MUSEUM IN PITTSBURGH. I WAS FORTUNATE ENUF (THANK YOU, ALLY!) TO BE INCLUDED IN THIS W/ PROPS FROM MY MOVIE "TEENAGERS FROM INNER SPACE". THE TINY TV SHOWED THE MOVIE & THE CASE TO THE RIGHT DISPLAYED THE PROPS.

HERE'S A LOOK AT MY SIDE OF THE CABINET & THEN A CLOSE-UP OF SOME OF THE PROPS - NOTE THE RECURRENCE OF JOKE-SHOP GAGS.

2008.05.03

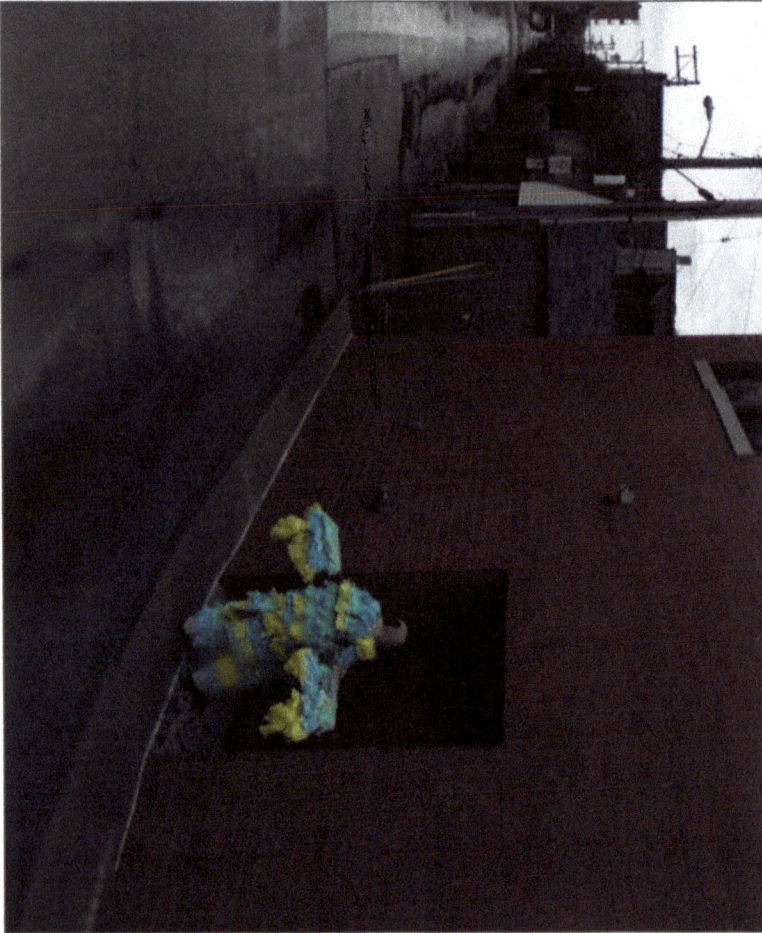

FOR WHAT SEEMED LIKE YRS THE CAR(S) W/ 360
DEGREE CAMERAS ON TOP WERE A COMMON SIGHT IN
PITTSBURGH. THEY ROAMED AROUND
SYSTEMATICALLY SHOOTING FOOTAGE OF PITTSBURGH
STREETS THAT CD THEN BE VIEWED ON GOOGLE
STREET VIEW ONLINE. ARTISTS ROBIN HEWLETT &
BEN KINSLEY HAD THE INSPIRED IDEA OF STAGING
HAPPENINGS IN THE VICINITY OF PITTSBURGH'S WONDERFUL
INSTALLATION MUSEUM THE MATTRESS FACTORY ON THE
NORTH SIDE AT A TIME WHEN THE STREET VIEW CAR WD BE
DRIVING THRU. I WAS INVITED TO PARTICIPATE SO I
PERFORMED VARIOUS ACTIONS WEARING THE ABOVE FEATHER-
DUSTER OUTFIT.

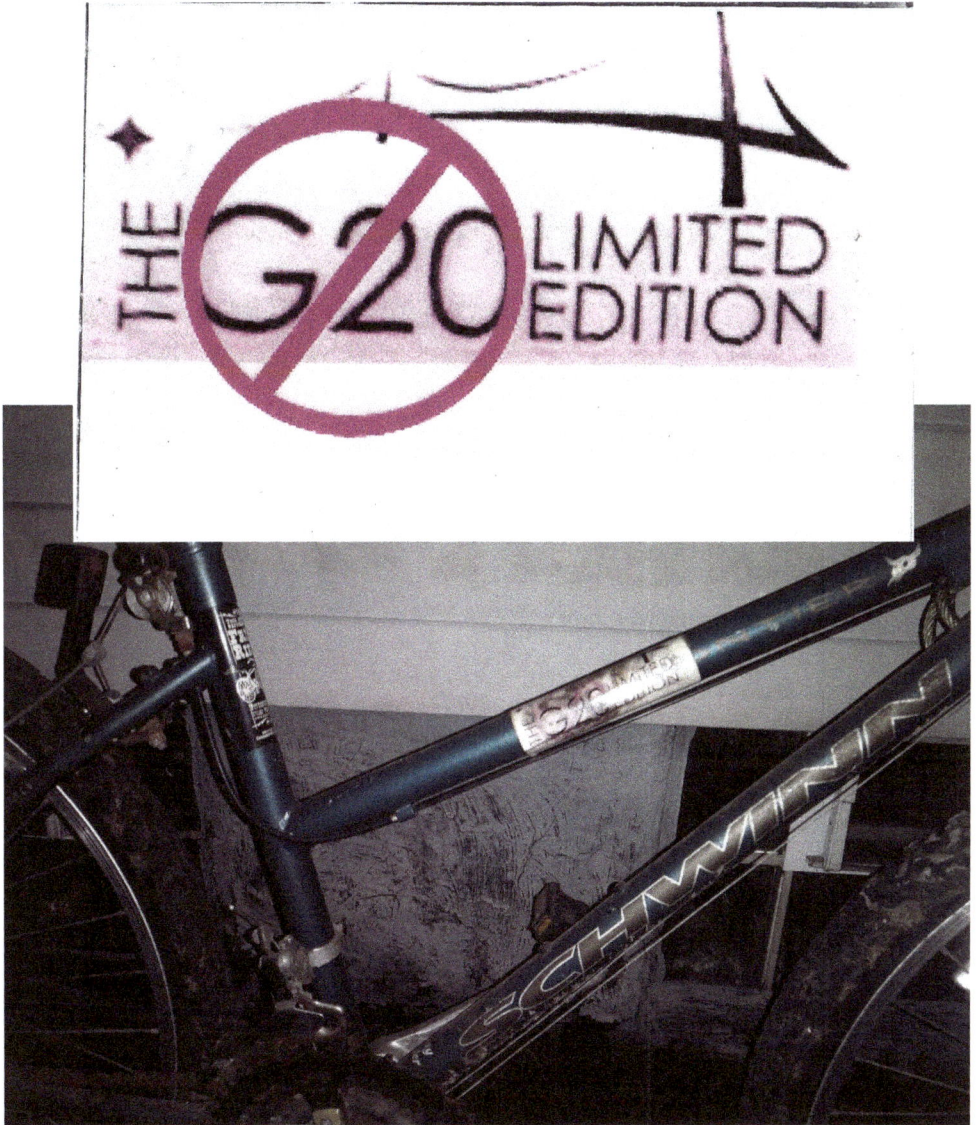

WHEN THE G20 CAME TO PITTSBURGH SO DID THE THUGS-IN-BLUE FROM ALL OVER THE COUNTRY. I GOT TO EXPERIENCE THE OCCUPYING ARMY THAT THE BLACK PANTHERS SO APTLY CRITICIZED - BUT IN MY NEIGHBORHOOD. SMITH & WESSON, THE ARMS MANUFACTURERS, MADE SPECIAL "G20 LIMITED EDITION" BIKES FOR THE COPS. I SHIT YOU NOT. I PHOTOGRAPHED THEIR BIKE STICKERS & MADE MY OWN ANTI-G20 STICKER TO PUT ON MY BIKE (SHOWN HERE MUCH THE WORSE FOR WEAR 14+ YRS LATER) & TO GIVE TO FRIENDS TO PUT ON THEIRS.

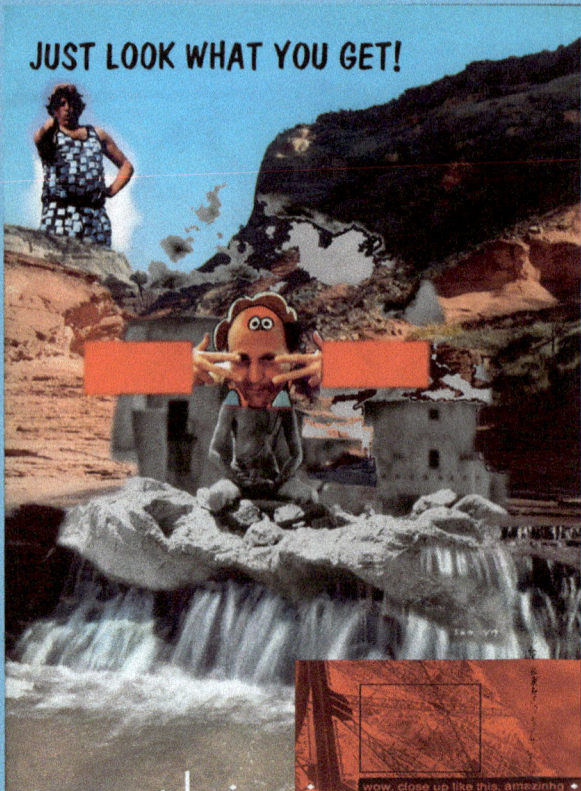

JUST LOOK WHAT YOU GET!

wow, close up like this, amazing
detail

wow, this is amazing

Paula Gillen & I both moved around alot & probably
didn't see each other from 1986 to 2010. But, somehow,
we got back in touch, possibly in 2009 by email, & I was
eager to rebuild our creative relationship. It must've
been around this time that I put together 3 programs
from my **ARCHIVE** of movies by friends & I started
shopping them around to screen. I succeeded in
screening all 3, the 3rd one twice. Apparently, I asked
Paula if she'd make an image advertising the screenings
& provided her w/ a couple images of me. The above is the
most elaborate one & the image on the following page
is a variation. Paula's sense of humor & taste for the
colorful shines thru.

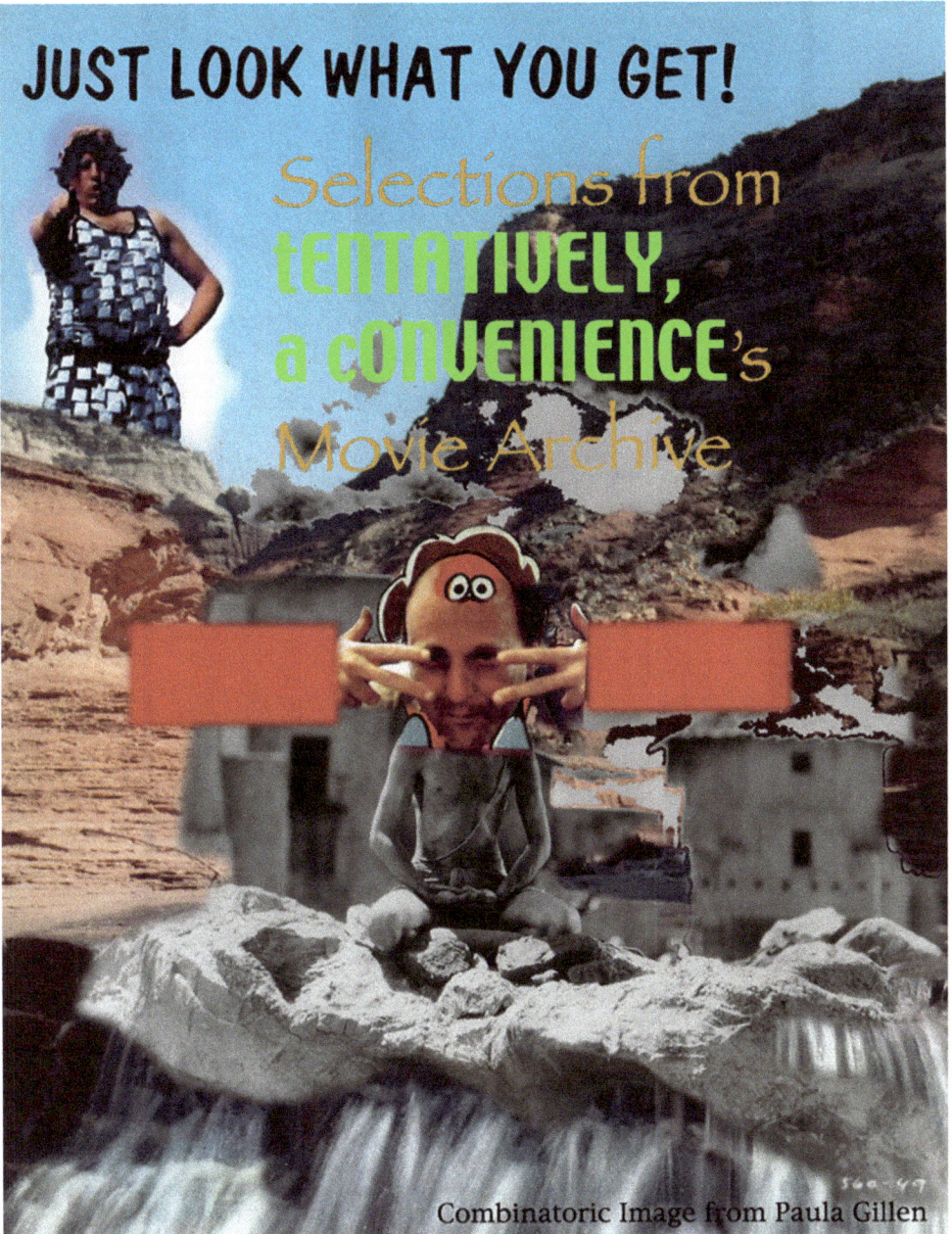

JUST LOOK WHAT YOU GET!

Selections from
tENTATIVELY,
a cONVENIENCE's
Movie Archive

Combinatoric Image from Paula Gillen

equation generating modules that I had designed. Each one produced its results using the 'tENT aTTRACTOR,' one of the simplest of chaotic equations. The nice thing about the tENT aTTRACTOR is that although it is wildly unpredictable, it also can swoop into doing repeating or very similar patterns from time to time ...

"For *Elegy*, I used four chaotic

"WE, LIKE SALANGAN SWALLOWS..."
A CHORAL GALLERY OF MORTON FELDMAN AND CONTEMPORARIES

MORTON FELDMAN
WILL OGDEN
EARLE BROWN
PAULINE OLIVEROS
WARREN BURT
ROBERT CARL

THE ASTRA CHOIR

COMPACT

Main
Carnegie Library of Pittsburgh

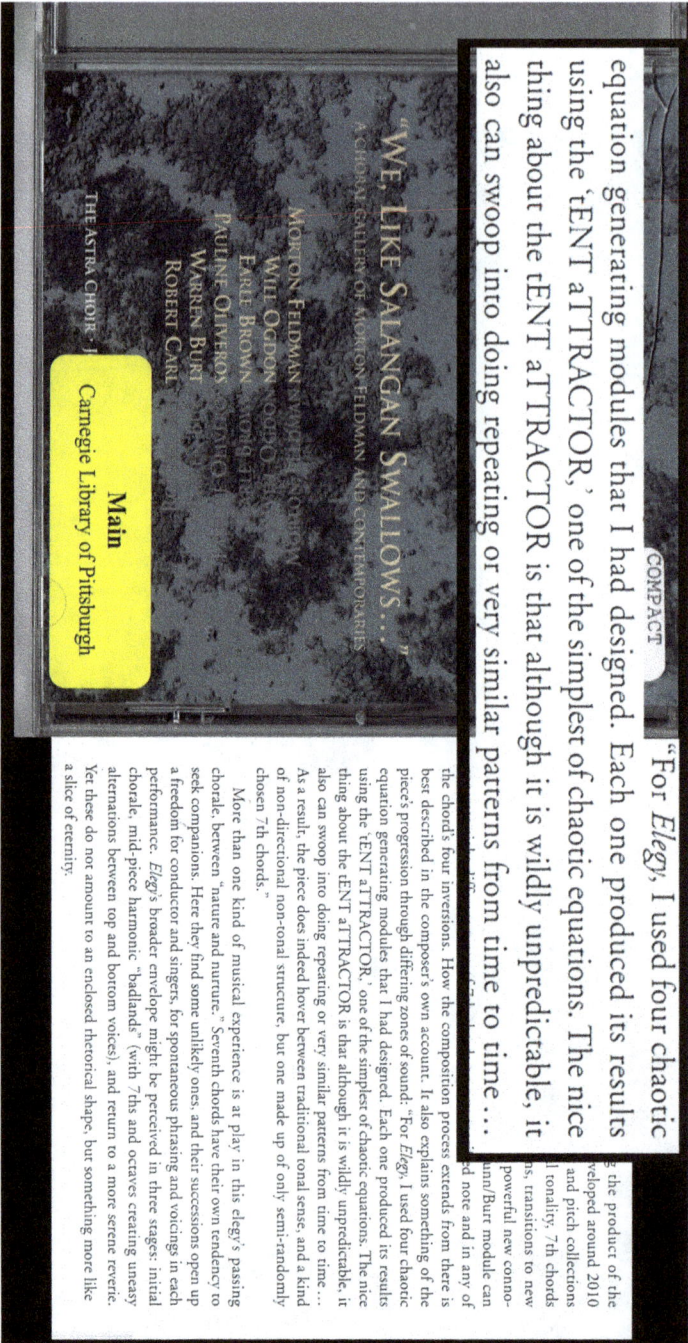

the chord's four inversions. How the composition process extends from there is best described in the composer's own account. It also explains something of the piece's progression through differing zones of sound: "For *Elegy*, I used four chaotic equation generating modules that I had designed. Each one produced its results using the 'tENT aTTRACTOR,' one of the simplest of chaotic equations. The nice thing about the tENT aTTRACTOR is that although it is wildly unpredictable, it also can swoop into doing repeating or very similar patterns from time to time ... As a result, the piece does indeed hover between traditional tonal sense, and a kind of non-directional non-tonal structure, but one made up of only semi-randomly chosen 7th chords."

More than one kind of musical experience is at play in this elegy's passing chorale, between "nature and nurture." Seventh chords have their own tendency to seek companions. Here they find some unlikely ones, and their successions open up a freedom for conductor and singers, for spontaneous phrasing and voicings in each performance. *Elegy*'s broader envelope might be perceived in three stages: initial chorale, mid-piece harmonic "badlands" (with 7ths and octaves creating uneasy alternations between top and bottom voices), and return to a more serene reverie. Yet these do not amount to an enclosed rhetorical shape, but something more like a slice of eternity.

g the product of the
veloped around 2010
and pitch collections
l tonality, 7th chords
ns, transitions to new
powerful new conno-
unn/Burt module can
d note and in any of

MY FRIEND IN AUSTRALIA, THE COMPOSER / MUSICIAN / IMPROVISOR / WRITER / MOVIEMAKER WARREN BURT, WAS KIND ENUF TO NAME SOME SOFTWARE AFTER ME & TO REFER TO ITS USE IN A CD'S LINER NOTES.

Long Live Larry Lawnchair!
- Shayn Fargesn - May, 2011 E.V.

[A FRIEND OF MINE HAD PLANNED TO PUBLISH A TRIBUTE TO LARRY LAWNCHAIR IN A BK WRAPPED IN WEATHER BALLOON MATERIAL. ALAS, THE PROJECT NEVER CAME TO FRUITION. THE FOLLOWING IS WHAT I WROTE FOR IT. SOMETHING THAT I DON'T WANT TO GO TO WASTE. "SHAYN FARGESN" IS ONE OF MY MANY NAMES - LOOK IT UP & YOU'LL UNDERSTAND IF YOU DON'T ALREADY.]

I DON'T KNOW WHEN I 1ST LEARNED ABOUT LARRY LAWNCHAIR'S ASTOUNDING ADVENTURE BUT I THINK IT MIGHT'VE BEEN THRU THE "NEWS OF THE WEIRD". I'VE BEEN IN THE NotW & SO HAS A GIRLFRIEND OF MINE. I THOUGHT THAT BOTH OF THE ACTIONS THAT EARNED US SUCH REPRESENTATIONS WERE SIGNS OF OUR EXCEPTIONAL LIVES. & I FELT THE SAME WAY ABOUT LL. I WANTED TO MEET HIM. MANY YRS LATER, I EVEN WROTE TO THE NEWS OF THE WEIRD PROPOSING THAT THEY HAVE SOME SORT OF REUNION FOR THE MORE CREATIVE PEOPLE WHO'VE APPEARED UNDER ITS BANNER - SUGGESTING THAT IT WD BE BOTH FUN & A FANTASTIC PUBLICITY STUNT. I NEVER GOT A REPLY.

ALAS, IT SEEMS TO'VE BECOME TYPICAL OF NotW FOR MANY PEOPLE PRESENTED BY IT TO BE USED AS EXAMPLES OF WEIRD = DUMB &/OR REPREHENSIBLE WCH I'D SAY IS DEFINITELY NOT ALWAYS THE CASE. BUT MAYBE LARRY WASN'T EVEN IN THE NotW. HE'S DEFINITELY A RECIPIENT OF A DARWIN AWARD - WCH IS EVEN SNARKIER. THE DARWIN AWARD OUTRIGHT SAYS THAT ANY RECIPIENTS THEREOF ARE STUPID & DESERVE TO BE WEEDED OUT OF THE GENE POOL. OF COURSE, AS IT SO OFTEN IS W/ SUCH 'REPORTAGE' DEPENDENT ON THE APPEAL OF SENSATIONAILISM, FAIRNESS & ACCURACY GOES BY THE WAYSIDE IN THE INTEREST OF UNITING THE COWARDLY HERD HUMANS AGAINST DIFFERENT PEOPLE TURNED INTO SCAPEGOATS.

2011.05

THE WEIRD = DUMB THING IS AKIN TO OUTSIDER = NAIVE WCH I'D SAY IS ALSO NOT ALWAYS THE CASE. FOR ME, LARRY LAWNCHAIR WAS A VISIONARY HERO. OF COURSE, I DIDN'T KNOW HIM PERSONALLY & I RECKON THAT IF I DID I'D HAVE A MORE COMPLEX PERCEPTION OF HIM.

AS THE READER MAY ALREADY 'KNOW', LARRY COMMITTED SUICIDE - SUPPOSEDLY NEVER ABLE TO READJUST TO 'NORMAL' LIFE AFTER SOARING FOR HUNDREDS OF MILES IN HIS WEATHER BALLOON LIFTED LAWNCHAIR. & WHY SHD HE HAVE ADJUSTED?! AS I RECALL, HE WAS A TRUCK-DRIVER, OR SOME SUCH - WCH MAY NOT'VE BEEN THE MOST EXCITING LIFE FOR HIM. AFTER HAVING THE EXTRAORDINARY EXPERIENCE OF FLYING AS HE DID, WHY WDN'T HE'VE FELT A NEED FOR CONTINUING TO LIVE OUTSIDE HUMDRUM ORDINARY LIFE?! HIS SUICIDE MAY'VE BEEN BOTH CONNECTED TO HIS 'INABILITY' (OR, MORE LIKELY, UNWILLINGNESS) TO READAPT TO THE MEDIOCRE AS WELL AS IN RESPONSE TO THE DEPRESSINGNESS OF PEOPLE RESPONDING TO HIS INCREDIBLE ACHIEVEMENT AS A SIGN OF HIS BEING A 'FOOL' - SOMETHING PROBABLY REINFORCED BY THINGS LIKE THE DARWIN AWARD & NEWS OF THE WEIRD.

LARRY'S WEATHER-BALLOON ASSISTED FLIGHT HAS ALWAYS RESONATED W/ ME IN VARIOUS WAYS: THE MOST OBVIOUS ONE BEING JUST IDENTIFICATION W/ THE BASIC HUMAN DESIRE TO FLY ACCOMPLISHED IN SUCH A NOVEL WAY; 2NDLY, I HAVE A THING FOR WEATHER BALLOONS. IN BALTIMORE, WHERE I'M FROM, THERE WAS A MILITARY SURPLUS STORE THAT SOLD WEATHER BALLOONS FAIRLY CHEAPLY & I WENT THRU A PERIOD IN MY LIFE IN THE 1970S WHEN THEY WERE COMMON OBJECTS FOR ME TO PLAY W/.

IN 1974 I LIVED IN AN APARTMENT IN DOWNTOWN BALTIMORE WHERE I HAD A SMALL BEDROOM W/ NO DOOR. TO CLOSE IT OFF, I PUT A WARDROBE'S BACK AGAINST THE DOORWAY FROM THE INSIDE OF THE ROOM & TOOK THE BACK OF PART OF THE WARDROBE OFF. TO ENTER THE ROOM, ONE HAD TO PUSH ASIDE

THE CLOTHES HANGING INSIDE THE WARDROBE. ENTER THRU THE HOLE IN THE BACK & UNDO THE WARDROBE'S DOOR FROM THE INSIDE. THIS WAS PROBABLY EVOCATIVE OF C.S.LEWIS' "THE LION, THE WITCH, & THE WARDROBE" - A FANTASY BK I WD'VE READ AS A CHILD THAT I'D PROBABLY ABHOR NOW FOR ITS HEAVY-HANDED CHRISTIAN SYMBOLISM.

INSIDE, THE ROOM WAS VERY SPARSE. I HAD A PIECE OF FOAM ON THE FLOOR AS MY BED, A LARGE DRAWING THAT I'D DONE ATTACHED TO THE WALL W/ STATIC ELECTRICITY, & AN INFLATED WEATHER BALLOON TAKING UP MOST OF THE SPACE - LEAVING, \PERHAPS, 2 FT ON EITHER SIDE OF ITS PERIMETER. AS SUCH, ENTERING THE ROOM BASICALLY INVOLVED NUDGING THE ELASTICITY OF THE LARGE BALLOON (PROBABLY INFLATED TO A 6 FT DIAMETER) & THEN EITHER STANDING ON THE ROOM'S EDGE OR SITTING ON THE FOAM. THE BALLOON PROBABLY REMINDED ME OF THE MYSTERIOUS ORB THAT PUSHED ATTEMPTED ESCAPEES BACK TO "THE VILLAGE" IN THE BRITISH TV SERIES "THE PRISONER" WCH I'D LIKED ALOT AS AN ADOLESCENT BEFORE I STOPPED WATCHING TV.

MY FRIEND & MAJOR COLLABORATOR, RICHARD ELLSBERRY, WHO PREFERRED TO JUST GO BY "RICHARD", WANTED TO INFLATE A SEX DOLL & FLY IT OVER MEMORIAL STADIUM, THE SPORTS ARENA IN BALTIMORE UNTIL THE 1990S. HE INFLATED THE SEX DOLL W/ HELIUM ONLY TO FIND THAT IT WAS ENTIRELY TOO HEAVY TO FLY THAT WAY. IN AN ATTEMPT TO SOLVE THIS PROBLEM HE BEGAN TO REMOVE PARTS OF THE DOLL THAT CD BE REMOVED W/O PUNCTURING A HOLE IN THE MAIN BODY. HENCE, THE BREASTS WENT 1ST. THIS, OBVIOUSLY, BEGAN TO PUT AN UNINTENDED SEX MUTILATION SPIN ON THE PROJECT. REGARDLESS OF HOW MUCH HE REMOVED, THE DOLL STILL WDN'T FLY SO HE HAD TO ABANDON THIS.

AT SOME POINT, PERHAPS IN THE EARLY 1980S, PROBABLY WHEN STAN VANDERBEEK WAS STILL ALIVE & TEACHING AT UMBC, CHARLOTTE MOORMAN WAS BROUGHT TO THE INNER HARBOR OF B-MORE IN AN ATTEMPT TO HAVE HER SENT ALOFT

2011.05

VIA WEATHER BALLOONS WHILST PLAYING CELLO. THIS MIGHT'VE BEEN A PROJECT OF NAM JUNE PAIK'S. THIS, TOO, FAILED B/C OF AN UNDERESTIMATION OF THE AMT OF HELIUM BALLOONS NEEDED.

AGAIN, IN THE 1980s, MY FRIEND & ANOTHER MAJOR COLLABORATOR DOUG RETZLER INITIATED SKY ART PROJECTS. DURING ONE OF THE "AD HOC FIASCOS" THAT HE & RICHARD WERE THE PRIME ORIGINATORS OF, DOUG LAUNCHED A LARGE (PERHAPS 20' X 4') PAINTING OF CLOUDS ON A LIGHT FABRIC (PERHAPS CHEESECLOTH) USING HELIUM FILLED BALLOONS. THIS PAINTING WAS ANCHORED TO THE GROUND BUT IT BROKE AWAY & FLOATED OFF. DOUG PANICKED, AFRAID THAT IT WD CAUSE AN AIR TRAFFIC ACCIDENT BY GETTING ENTANGLED IN THE PROPS OF A SMALL PLANE OR IN JET ENGINES OR WHAT-HAVE-YOU. HE PHONED THE FAA & TOLD THEM HIS STORY & THEY BASICALLY TOLD HIM NOT TO WORRY ABOUT IT - SAYING THAT THE ODDS AGAINST SUCH AN ACCIDENT WERE ASTRONOMICAL.

DURING ANOTHER AD HOC FIASCO, DOUG LAUNCHED A FIBERGLASS STATUE THAT HE'D MADE OF A LIFESIZED HUMAN HOLDING A VIDEO CAMERA THAT WAS CABLE-TETHERED TO THE GROUND SO THAT THE CAMERA'S ARIAL PERSPECTIVE CD BE SEEN ON A TV THAT THE CABLE WAS PLUGGED INTO (DISPLAYED IN AN RV'S WINDOW).

MY FAVORITE DOUG STORY ALONG THESE LINES WAS FROM WHEN HIS 1ST CHILD WAS BORN IN 1988. DOUG DECIDED THAT HE WANTED THE CHILD TO UNDERGO EXTRAORDINARY EXPERIENCES IN ITS 1ST 2 WKS SO HE PUT THE BABY IN A CAR SEAT & SENT IT ALOFT, TETHERED OF COURSE, W/ ITS POINT OF ORIGIN BEING THE TREE THAT HE & HIS WIFE HAD JUST PLANTED IN THE HOLE WHERE THEY'D BURIED THE BABY'S PLACENTA [ACTUALLY, IT WAS AN OCTOPUS - THE HOSPITAL THREW OUT THE PLACENTA]! THE PICTURE BELOW SHOWS THE BABY ALOFT. THE BABY WAS 5 DAYS OLD.

Many yrs later, an Australian director made a movie inspired by Larry Lawnchair called "Danny Deckchair". The story roughly paralleled Larry's own except that Danny's life had a happy romantic comedy ending. If only Larry's had had the same.

Larry Lawnchair is Dead!, Long Live Larry Lawnchair!

PAULA GILLEN CROPS UP AGAIN - THIS TIME W/ HER SCULPTURES USED IN MY MOVIE "COLONY". PHOTO TAKEN BY PAULA.

That's all well & good. However, we can make a trickier statement:

tENTATIVELY, a cONVEN IENCE

SELECTED SHORTS 2000-2011

From "Haircut Paradox", '05-06

WED, FEB 22 @ 7PM

Pink House Studio

601 E. Wright St. / Riverwest

Presented by Light Stroke + Milwaukee Underground FF

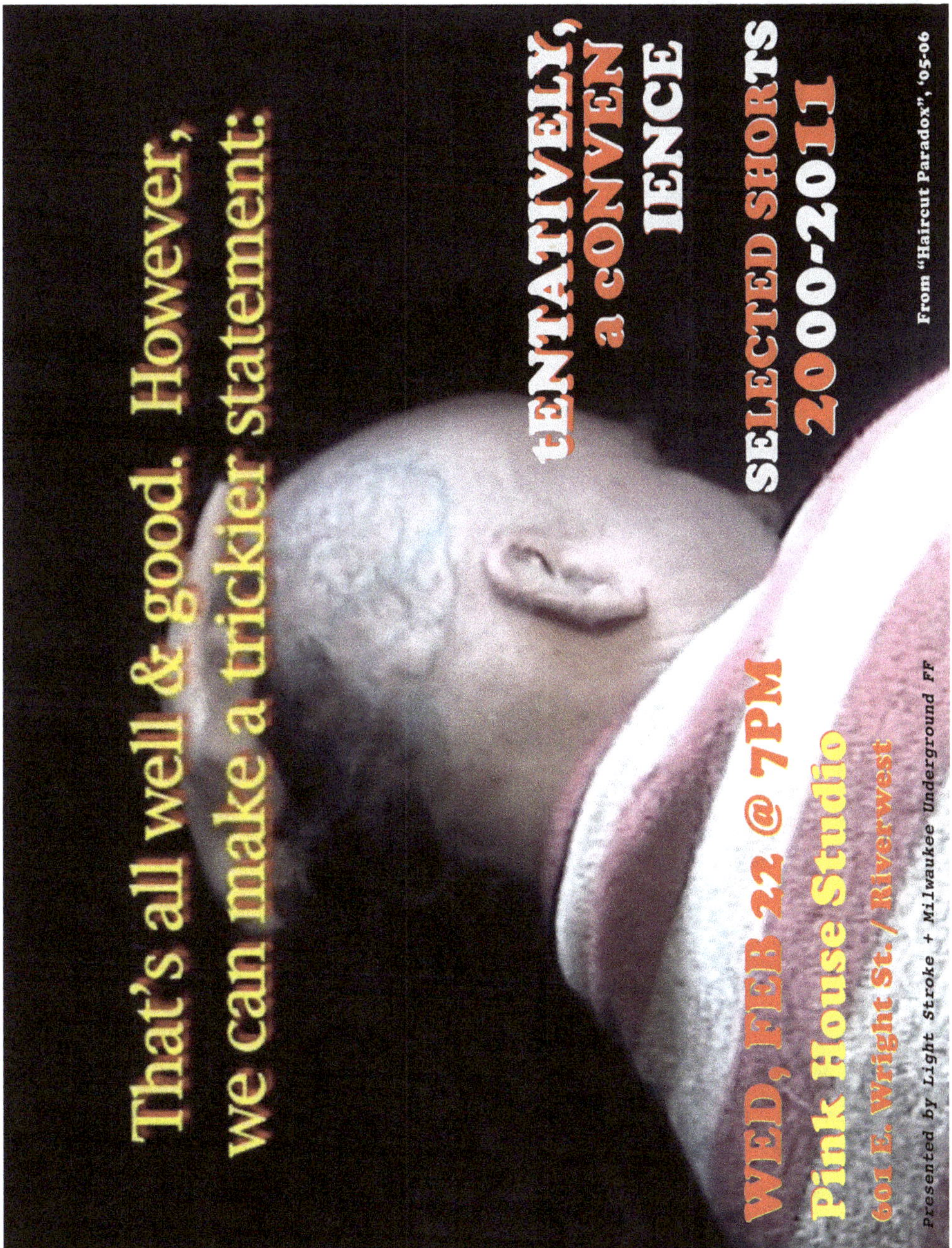

THIS IS FROM MILWAUKEE. THE SHOW WAS SET UP BY ROSS NUGENT (THANKS ROSS!). THERE WAS A TIME WHEN I CD PRESENT MY WORK SOMEWHAT WIDELY. GEE, I WONDER WHAT HAPPENED?!

2013.07.17

The backyard of my house was a jungle of knotweed & wild grape when I bought it in 2006. Since it was more or less 'impenetrable' I started attacking it, w/ only temporary 'success'. By 2013 I put in 4 concrete pads w/ vinyl records 'growing' out of them. My intention was to conjoin the 4 record columns into an arbor that the grape vines cd grow on. The idea was that the vine tendrils wd 'play' the records. I called it "I Heard It Through the Grapevine". I never finished it.

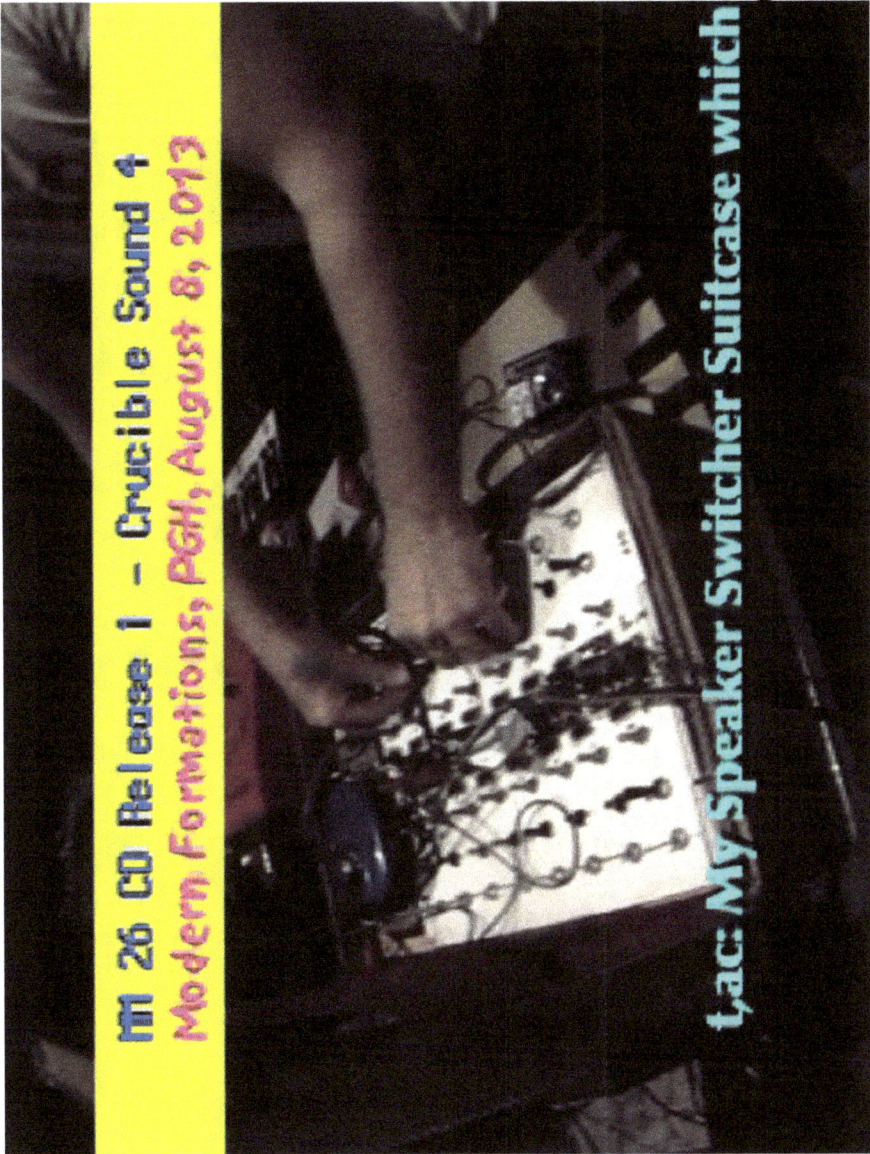

MM 26 CD Release 1 - Crucible Sound 4
Modern Formations, PGH, August 8, 2013

t,ac: My Speaker Switcher Suitcase which

I BUILT MY "SPEAKER SWITCHER SUITCASE" IN 1992. IT ONLY
HALF-WORKED & WASN'T THAT GREAT TO BEGIN W/ BUT AS AN
AMBITIOUS MASS OF TINY WIRING IT WAS AN ACCOMPLISHMENT
FOR ME. I HAVEN'T USED IT MUCH BUT I DID BREAK IT OUT FOR
THE 1ST OF 2 RELEASES FOR THE "MM 26" COMPILATION CD
THAT I PUBLISHED. THE ABOVE STILL IS FROM THE MOVIE I
MADE OF THAT EVENT.

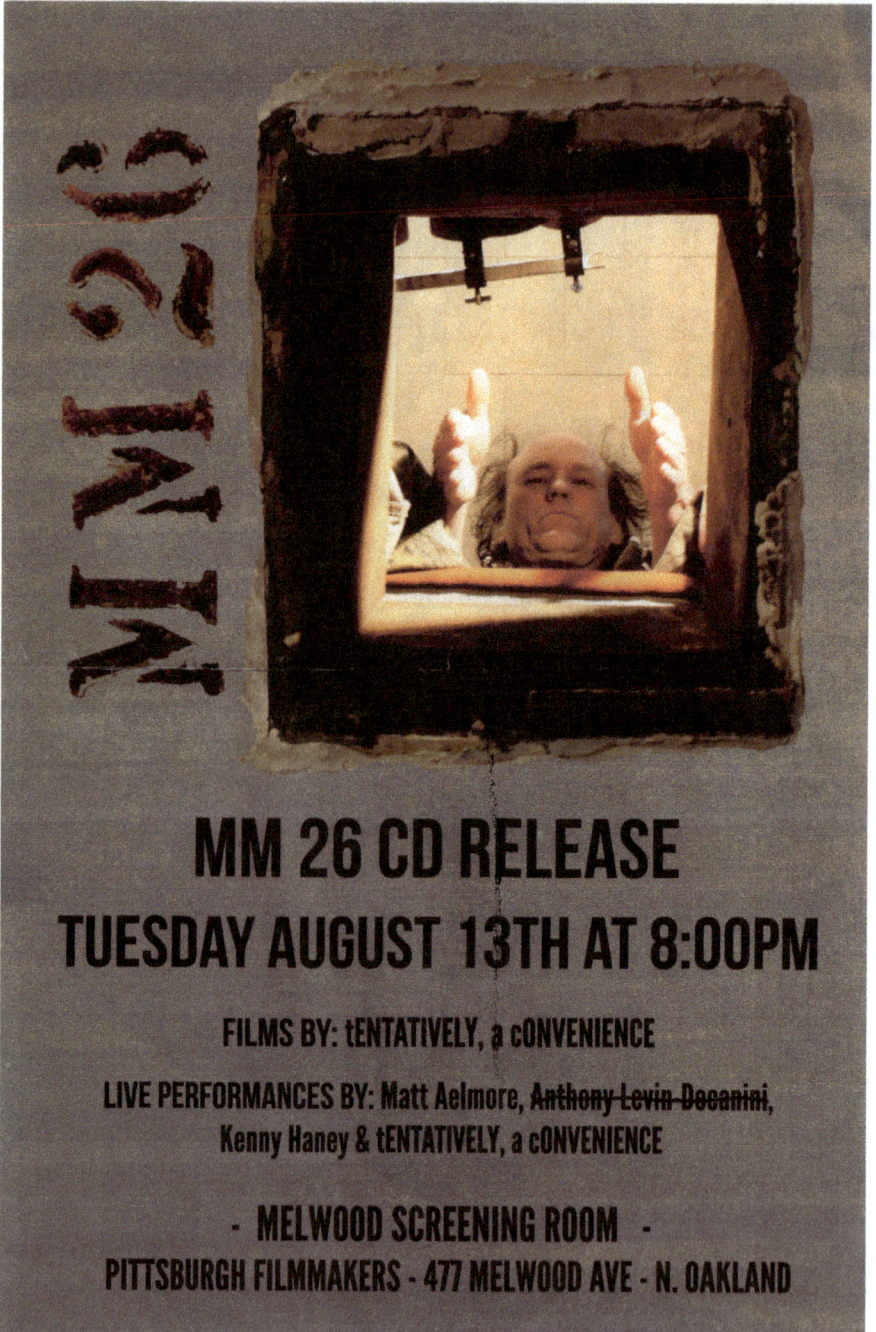

MM 26 CD RELEASE
TUESDAY AUGUST 13TH AT 8:00PM

FILMS BY: tENTATIVELY, a cONVENIENCE

LIVE PERFORMANCES BY: Matt Aelmore, ~~Anthony Levin Decanini~~,
Kenny Haney & tENTATIVELY, a cONVENIENCE

- MELWOOD SCREENING ROOM -
PITTSBURGH FILMMAKERS - 477 MELWOOD AVE - N. OAKLAND

THIS IS THE POSTER FOR THE 2ND OF THE TWO "MM 26" CD
RELEASE EVENTS. I PROBABLY PROVIDED THE IMAGE (IT'S ME
LOOKING THRU A HOLE IN THE FLOOR OF MY HOUSE) BUT
SOMEONE ELSE MIGHT'VE DESIGNED THE POSTER.

2013.11.01

I WORKED FOR A NATURAL HISTORY MUSEUM FOR ALMOST A DECADE. THAT ENABLED ME TO FAKE SHOWING WHAT I THINK OF AS AN "ARCTIC PRAIRIE DOG" A MOVIE I MADE CALLED "COLONY" THAT FEATURES PRAIRIE DOGS IN BOULDER, CO, US@. THIS IMAGE THEN BECAME MY CHANNEL 'ART' FOR MY ONESOWNTHOUGHTS YOUTUBE CHANNEL.

I HAVE A LONG-STANDING LOVE FOR FLUXUS & HAVE HAD THE
HONOR & PLEASURE OF MEETING JOHN CAGE, DICK HIGGINS, &
ALISON KNOWLES. I'M STANDING W/ THE LATTER IN THIS PICTURE
IN THE RED GRID IN HER EXHIBIT AT THE CARNEGIE MUSEUM OF
ART IN PITTSBURGH. SHE'S HOLDING A RED CORDUROY FRAME OF
REFERENCE SHAPE FROM MY SALAD DRESSING THAT I GAVE HER.

THIS IS A TRUE CELLFIE. SELFIES ARE SUPERABUNDANT BUT HOW MANY PEOPLE DO ANYTHING IMAGINATIVE W/ THEM?

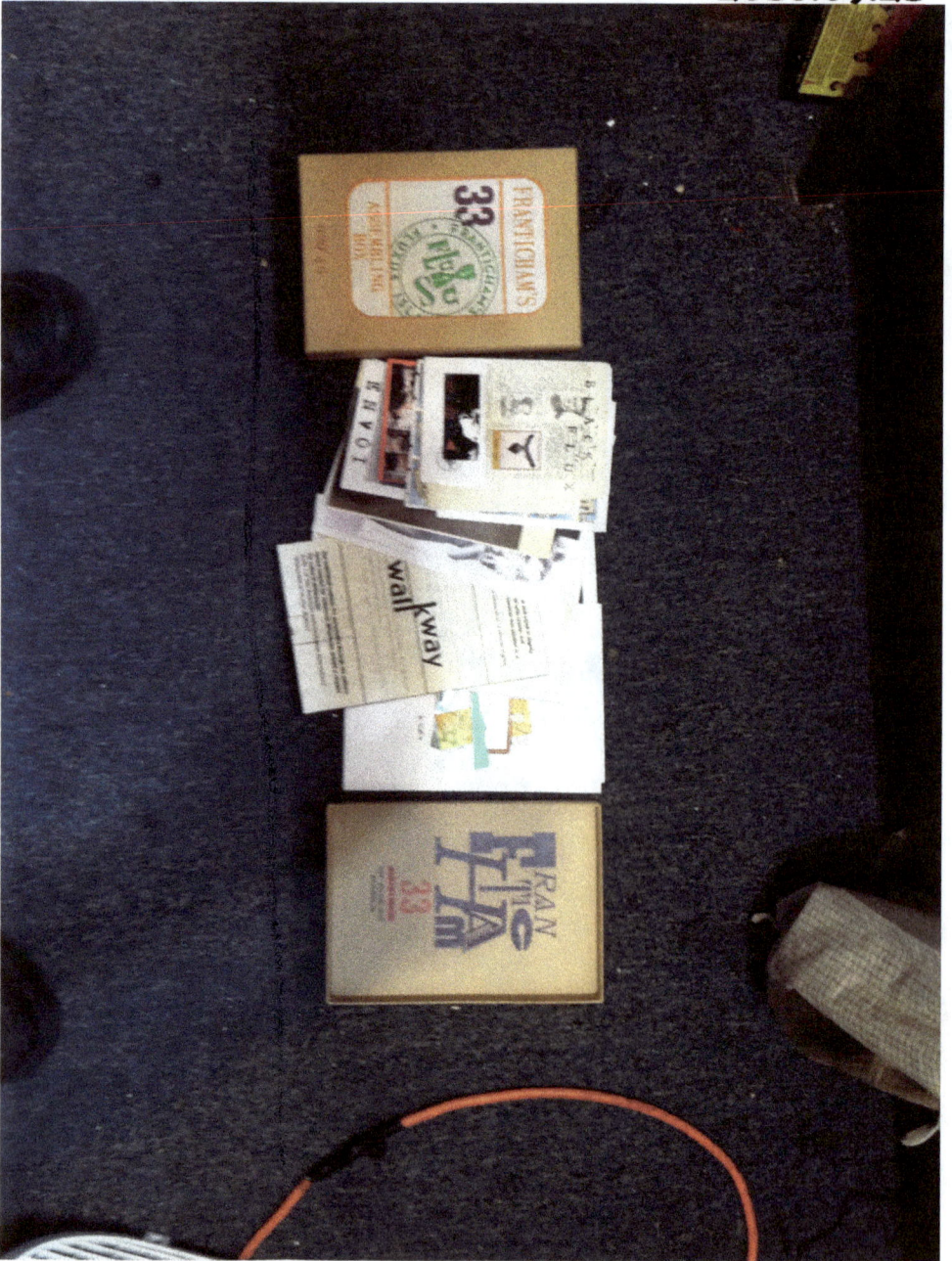

I LOVE ASSEMBLINGS & HOPE TO MAKE A MODEST MOVIE ABOUT
THE ONES IN MY ARCHIVE SOMEDAY SOON. HERE'S THE LAST
ONE I CONTRIBUTED TO. THE "WALKWAY" PIECE IN THE MIDDLE
IS MINE.

neoism

neoism?

MY FRIEND & FELLOW NEOIST CARRION ELITED (AKA MONTE CON
O SIN SAFOS) VISITED ME IN AUGUST OF 2016 & I MADE A MOVIE
ABOUT HIM. WE VISITED THE CENTER FOR POSTNATURAL
HISTORY WHERE THIS PICTURE WAS TAKEN OF ME W/ THE
TAXIDERMIED GENETICALLY-MODIFIED GOAT ON DISPLAY THERE.
CARRION TOOK THAT PICTURE & TURNED IT INTO THE ABOVE.

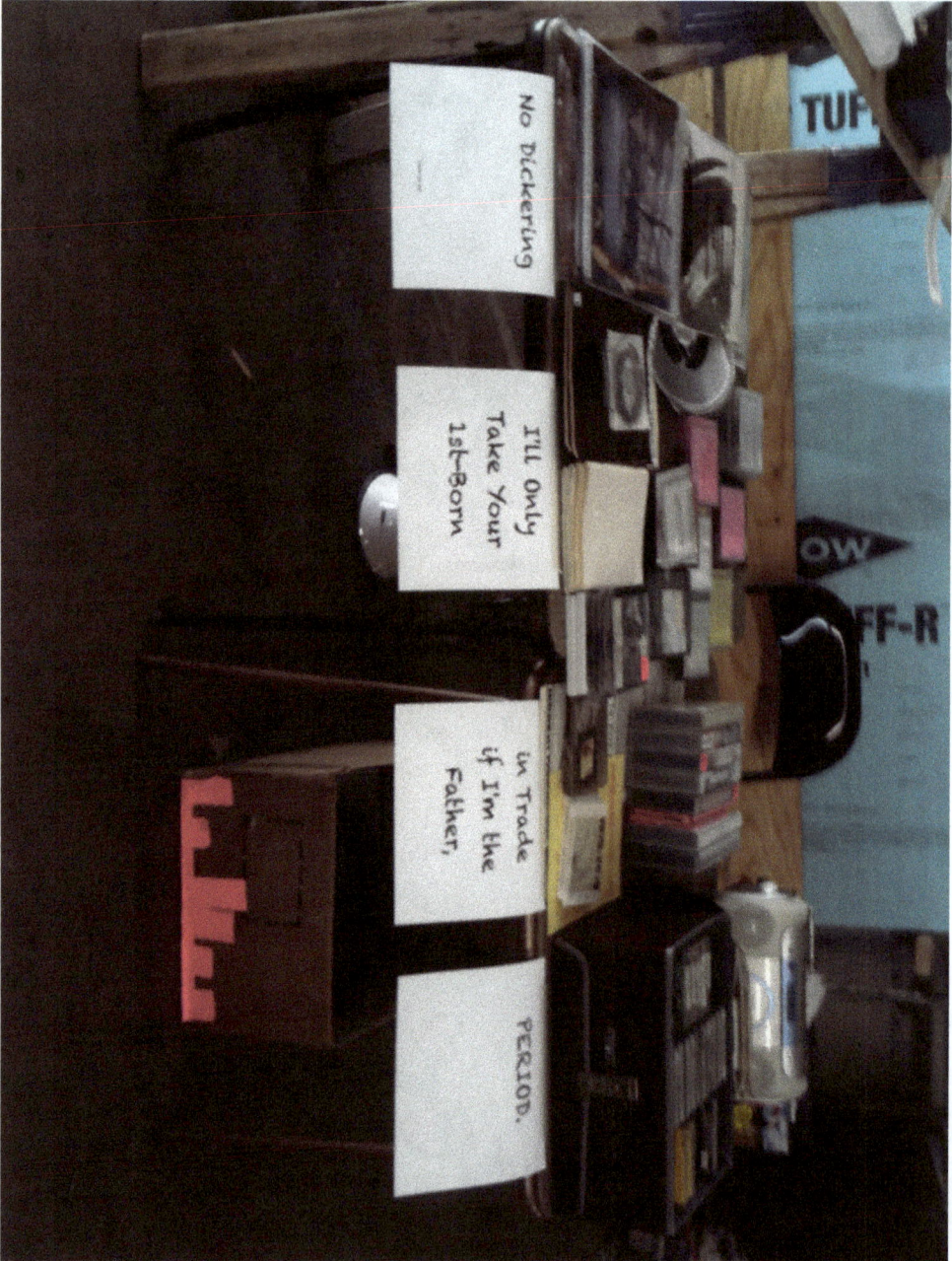

ONCE UPON A TIME I WAS CLOSE TO A CREW CALLED "BABYLAND" & CD TRY TO SELL MY MERCHANDISE AT THEIR PERIODIC SALES. HERE I TRY OUT MY OWN PERSONAL & PERSONABLE SALES TECHNIQUE. I MIGHT'VE EVEN SOLD A THING OR 2.

I WAS INVITED TO BE A PART OF A DUETS RECORDING PROJECT ORGANIZED BY THAT JUGGERNAUT OF THE HOME ELECTROACOUSTIC SCENE, [AN] EeL. HE PAIRED ME W/ MY OLD PAL MIEKAL AND & WE MADE A COLLABORATION CALLED "OWL PONG" WCH APPEARED ON BANDCAMP AS PART OF THE "TWO HALVES: VOLUME ONE" RELEASE.. THE ABOVE IS AN IMAGE I MADE FOR MY DOCUMENTARY OF MY MAKING MY "PING PONG" PART. THE DOC'S CALLED "MAKING DÜ". GWEN SADLER PROVIDED IJONES CAMERAWORK.

2018.03.14

IN 2018 I MADE A MOVIE EVERY DAY OF MY PLAYING (M)USIC. THAT DEVELOPED INTO SOMETHING EVEN MORE COMPLEX & DIFFICULT THAN MY ORIGINAL INTENTION. THE ABOVE STILL IS FROM THE MOVIE I MADE ON MARCH 14, 2018, IN WCH I WAS A QUINTET: LEFT-TO-RIGHT: SPINET. ELECTRIC GUITAR, ELECTRONICS, ALTO SAX, ERECTOR SET PERCUSSION.

If Christ was a prophet, is the Antichrist a non-profit?

BACK IN THE DAY WHEN I USED FECESBOOK, BEFORE I REJECTED ITS FUNCTION AS A PEER PRESSURE COOKER THAT DUMBS PEOPLE DOWN TO THE LEVEL OF AU (ARTIFICIAL UNINTELLIGENCE), I HAD SOME FUN USING THE PRE-FABRICATED BACKDROPS FOR GLIB STATEMENTS.

Once upon a time, people believed all sorts of stupid shit & sometimes it was fun but most of the time it was just a drag.

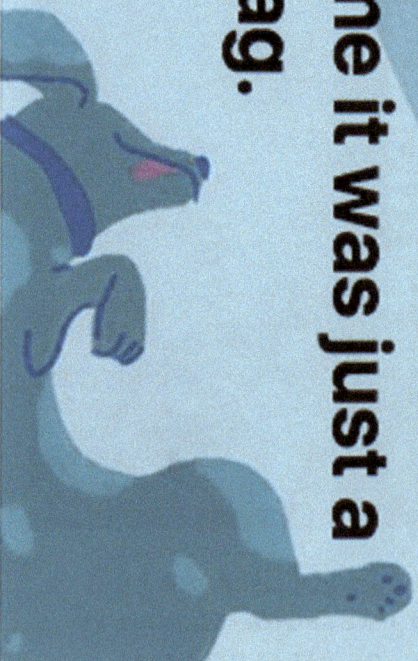

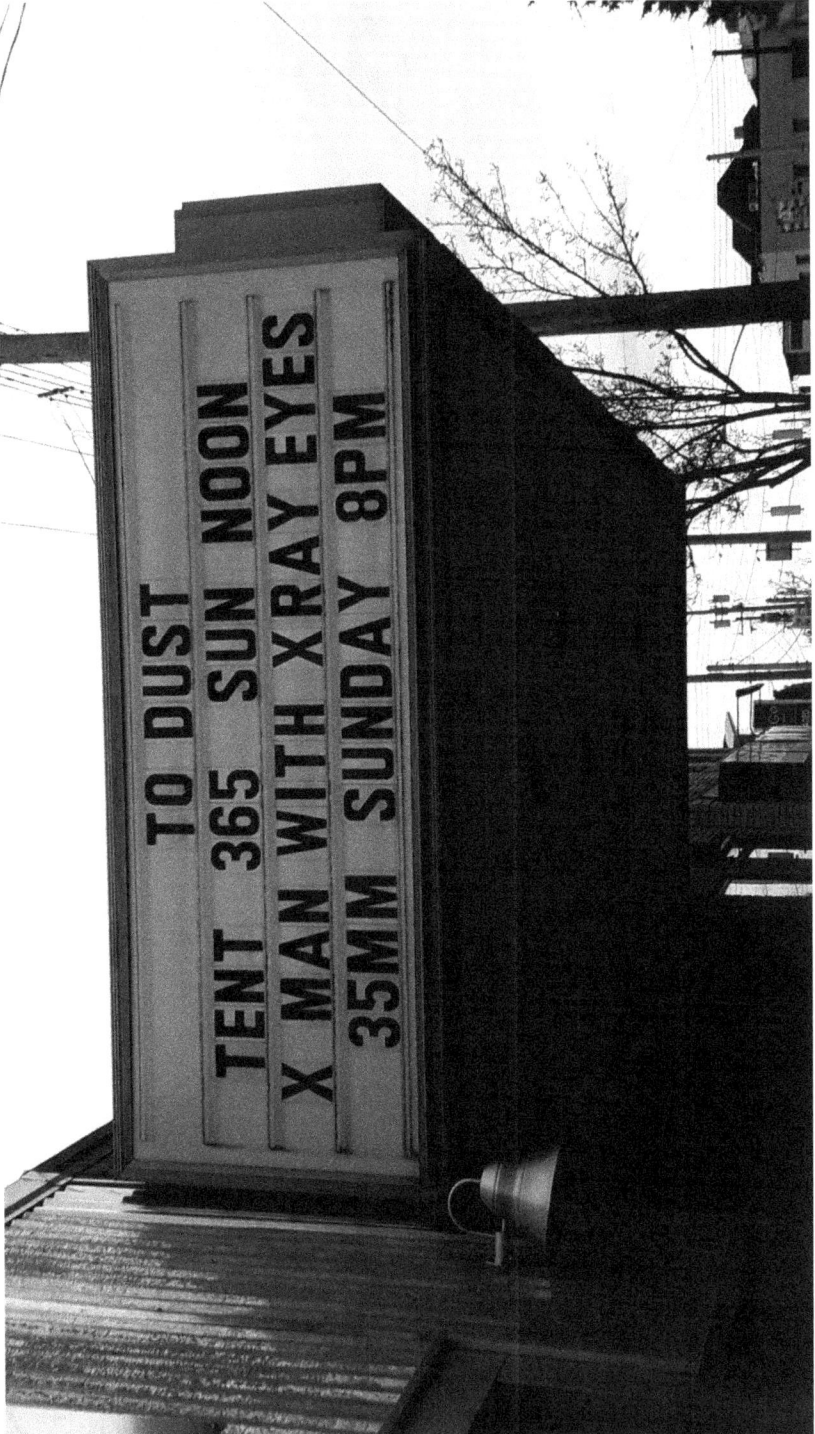

2019.04.07

TO DUST
TENT 365 SUN NOON
X MAN WITH X RAY EYES
35MM SUNDAY 8PM

2019.04.07

My 2018 project of daily (m)usic moviemaking turned into a feature movie called "365" wch turned into a score that was performed at the Regent Square Theater in Pittsburgh w/ 7 players. This image is from the documentary about that.

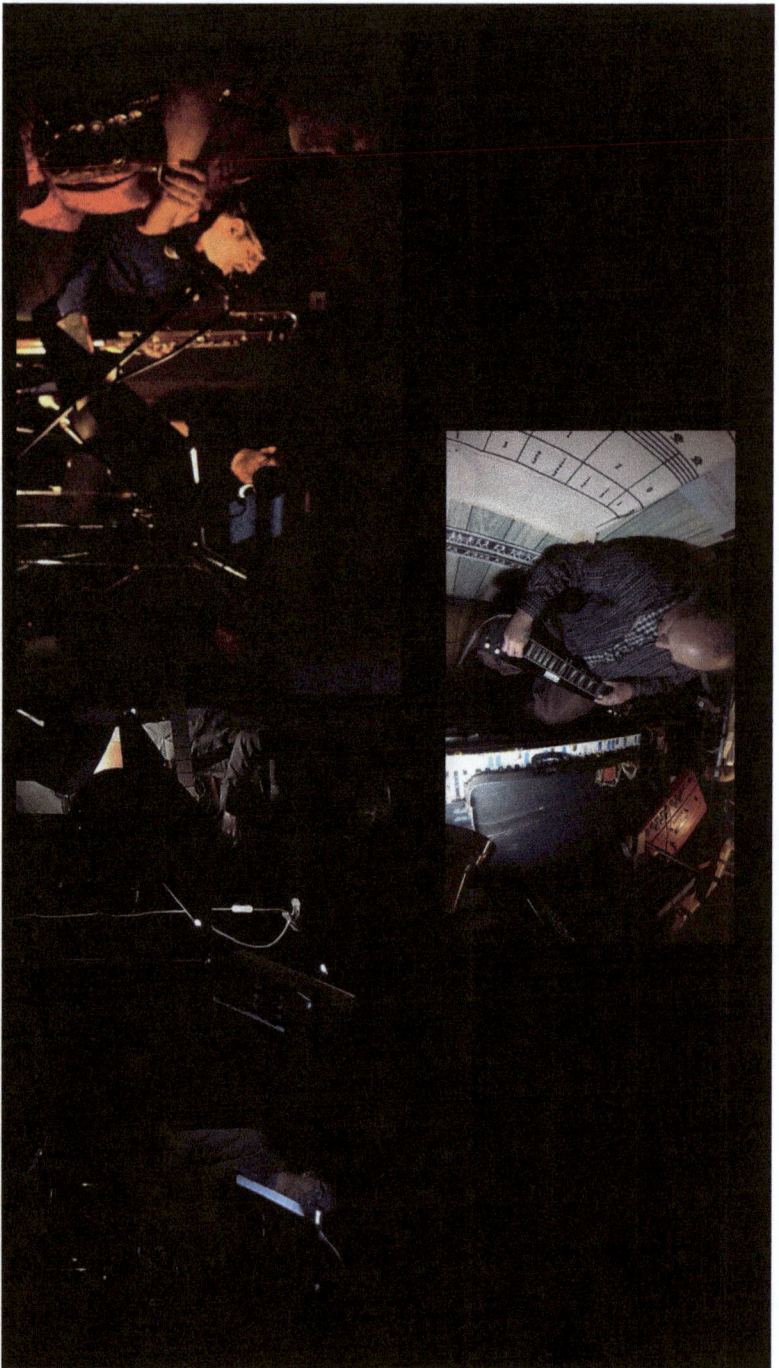

2019.04.14

As Neoism approaches its 40th it descends into police state madness with character assassination & purges.

ⓘ The listing you're looking for has ended.

Chakra -animation-1973- nomination Chicago
film festival -best short (no leader)

Condition: Good
Ended: May 27, 2019, 06:40:57 AM PDT
Price: US $90.00

We found something similar

70mm Film Cine Type II Perf White Leader
Standard Theatrical Format

FORTUNATELY FOR MY CRIMINAL SANITY, EVEN MARKETING ALGORITHMS CAN PROVIDE ME W/ A FEW GOOD LAUGHS FROM TIME-TO-TIME. THE ABOVE IS A GOOD EXAMPLE. I WAS LOOKING FOR A 16MM PRINT OF JORDAN BELSON'S FABULOUS MOVIE "CHAKRA". ALAS, THE PRINT I WAS THINKING OF BUYING SOLD. ANYONE WHO KNOWS BELSON'S WORK KNOWS HOW UTTERLY LUCIOUS & COLORFUL IT IS. WELL, WELL, RATHER THAN LEAVE ME DISATISFIED W/ NOT HAVING PURCHASED ANYTHING THE INTERNET CAME UP W/ AN ALTERNATIVE: WHITE LEADER.

I'M ONE OF THOSE STRANGE PEOPLE WHO ACTUALLY CARES ABOUT HAVING THEIR CONTRIBUTIONS TO THE WORLD, TO CULTURE, TO THE INTELLECTUAL GESTALT BECOME FIRMLY ESTABLISHED FOR POSTERITY TO OGLE ALL OVER. GYÖRGY GALANTAI OF ARTPOOL IN BYDAPEST DISPLAYS SOME OF THE THINGS I'VE DONATED TO THEIR ARCHIVE.

MODULATION

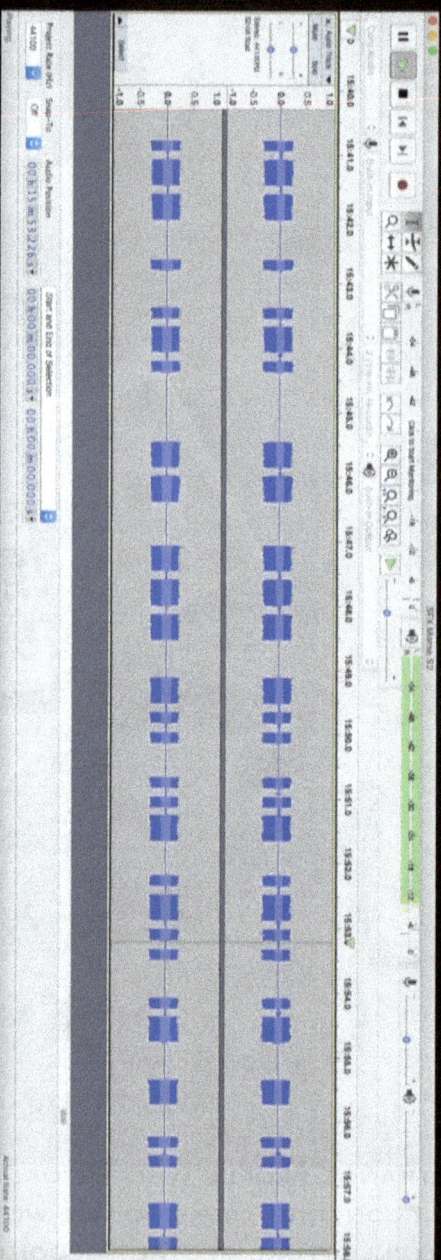

I'VE ALWAYS FOUND MORSE CODE INTERESTING EVEN THOUGH I'VE NEVER LEARNED IT. AS SUCH, I STARTED MAKING WORK USING IT W/ AN EAR TO HAVING IT FACTOR IN SOMEHOW TO PERFORMANCES BY MY NEW GROUP "THE TICKET THAT EXPLODED" NAMED AFTER THE WILLIAM S. BURROUGHS NOVEL THAT FOLLOWED "THE SOFT MACHINE".

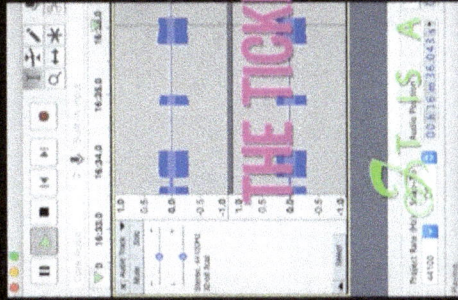

TICKET

THE TICKET THAT EXPLODED is a poetic license.

LICENSE TAKEN BY THOSE WHO USE IT.

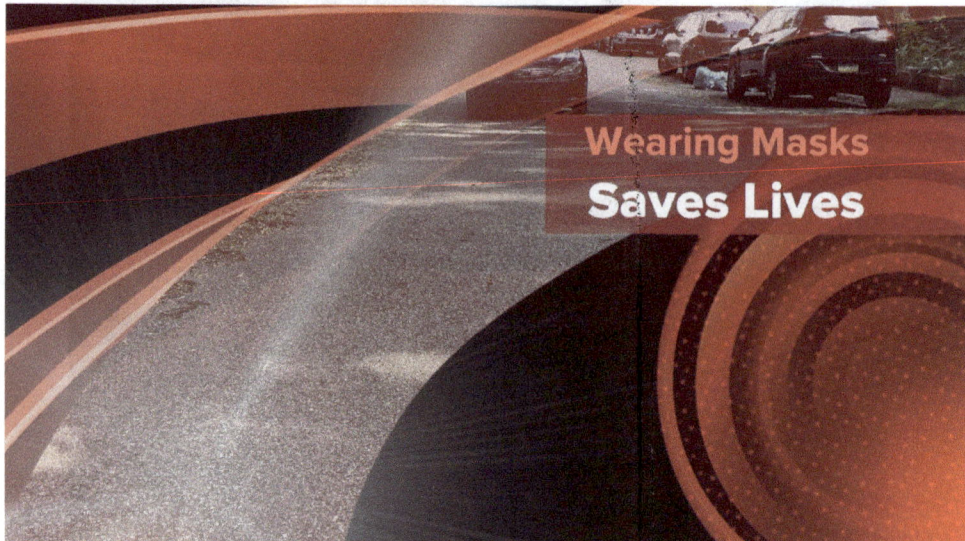

Wearing Masks
Saves Lives

2020 BROUGHT THE DIABOLICAL QUARANTYRANNY, A GROSSLY EXAGGERATED (OR ENTIRELY IMAGINARY) HEALTH 'EMERGENCY' THAT'S BEEN USED EVER SINCE TO PUT THE ROBOPATHS, THE SHEEPLE, IN THEIR PLACE & TO GIVE A NEW LEASE ON LIFE TO THE UNTERTANEN. I STARTED CRITICIZING THIS IN A LARGE VARIETY OF WAYS IMMEDIATELY. ONE WAS BY MAKING FUN OF MASK-WEARING. THIS WORK ISN'T LIKELY TO BE SHOWN ANYWHERE ANYTIME SOON. IT'S ALREADY BEEN REJECTED BY SOMEONE WHO OTHERWISE LIKES MY WORK. IT'S BEEN AGE-RESTRICTED ON YOUTUBE.

2020.07

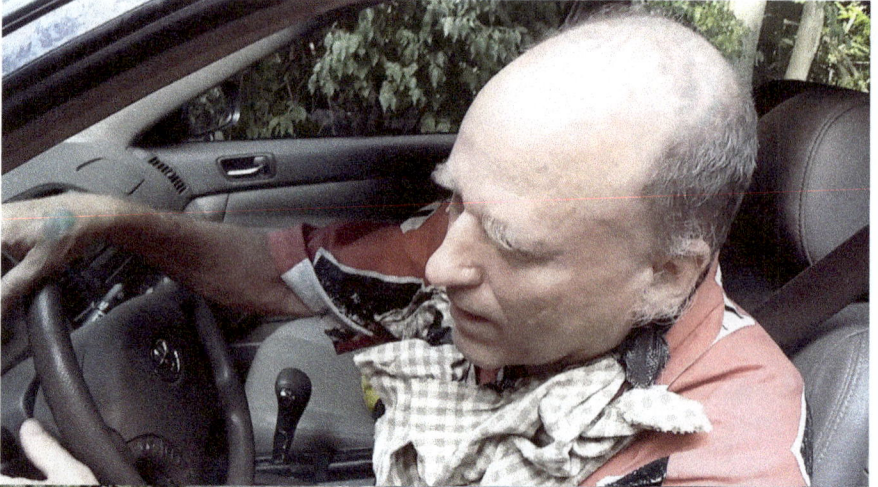

Not Wearing Masks Kills People

THE IMAGE I USED AT THE BOTTOM HERE WAS TAKEN FROM
THE INTERNET. IT WAS OF A DEAD PERSON. THE PEOPLE
INVOLVED IN MAKING THE IMAGE SEEMED TO HAVE A SENSE
OF HUMOR, MAYBE   THEY WDN'T MIND
MY USING THE IMAGE.   ALAS, I DECIDED TO,
UH, CROP IT UP A BIT   TO AVOID LEGAL
TROU-   BLES IMPEDING THE
PRO-   DUCTION OF THIS BK. SORRY
ABOUT   THAT. THE IDEA WAS TO SHOW A PERSON
MURDERED BY ME BY MY TAKING OFF MY MASK. RIGHT.

Or is it Masks Save Lives?

it Masks Save Lives?

THANKS TO BREEN CASEY FOR BEING THE PEDESTRIAN TOO ENGROSSED IN HER CELL PHONE TO NOTICE TRAFFIC.

HERETIC:
tENTATIVELY, a cONVENIENCE

I'm Anti-Quarantyranny
AND Anti-Racist.
They aren't Mutually Exclusive.

MAKE
ORWELL
FICTION
AGAIN

THE PROPAGANDISTS WERE HARD AT WORK CHARACTER
ASSASSINATING EVERYONE WHO HAD THE AUDACITY TO
GIVE A CRITICAL READING OF THE PUSH FOR MEDICAL
TOTALITARIANISM. HENCE, THROUGH SLIGHT-OF-MIND.
ANTI-MASK & ANTI-VAX BECAME RACIST! IT DIDN'T HAVE
TO MAKE ANY SENSE, IT JUST HAD TO SCARE PEOPLE INTO
CONFORMING OR RISK BEING SLANDERED & SHUNNED.

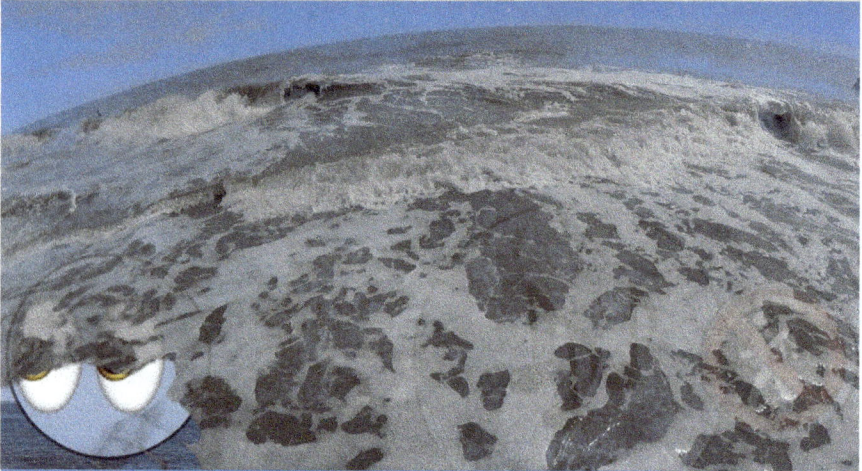

FOR MY 67TH BIRTHDAY I MADE "LIKE A DECOY OUT OF WATER".

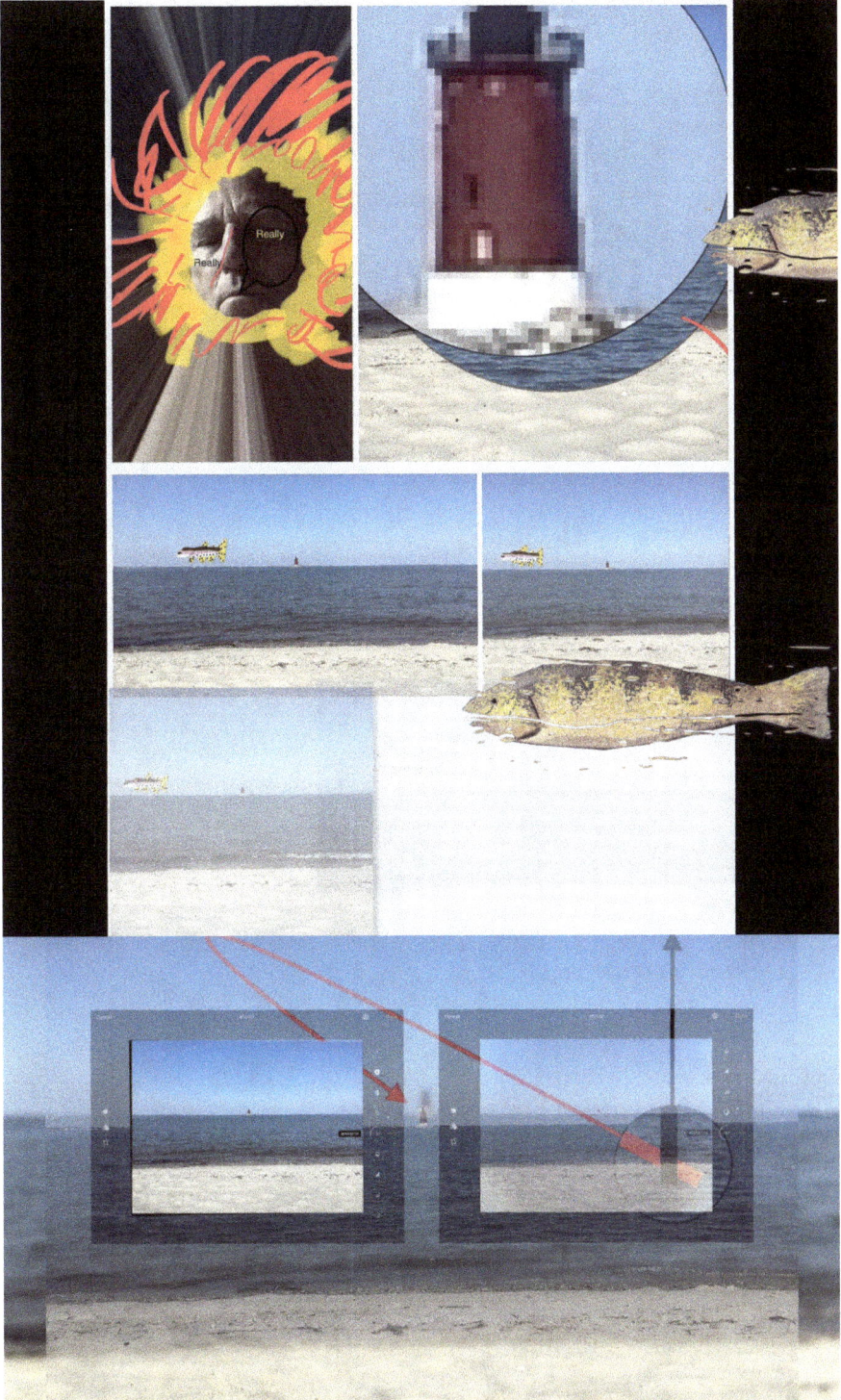

I EXPERIMENTED W/ AN IPUD FOR ANIMATIING. THAT WAS FUN.

For decades it seemed to me that Bud Light
was the litterer's choice because it was
the main trash I saw everywhere.

Now, in the time of the New Normality,
humanity has progressed!
Masks are the New Litter.
It's so good to see health consciousness
at work.

2021.01.26

THE ABOVE IS ACTUALLY A PICTURE OF THE PITTSBURGH SKY ON
THE DATE GIVEN. IT'S NOT POLLUTION, IT'S JUST CLOUDS.

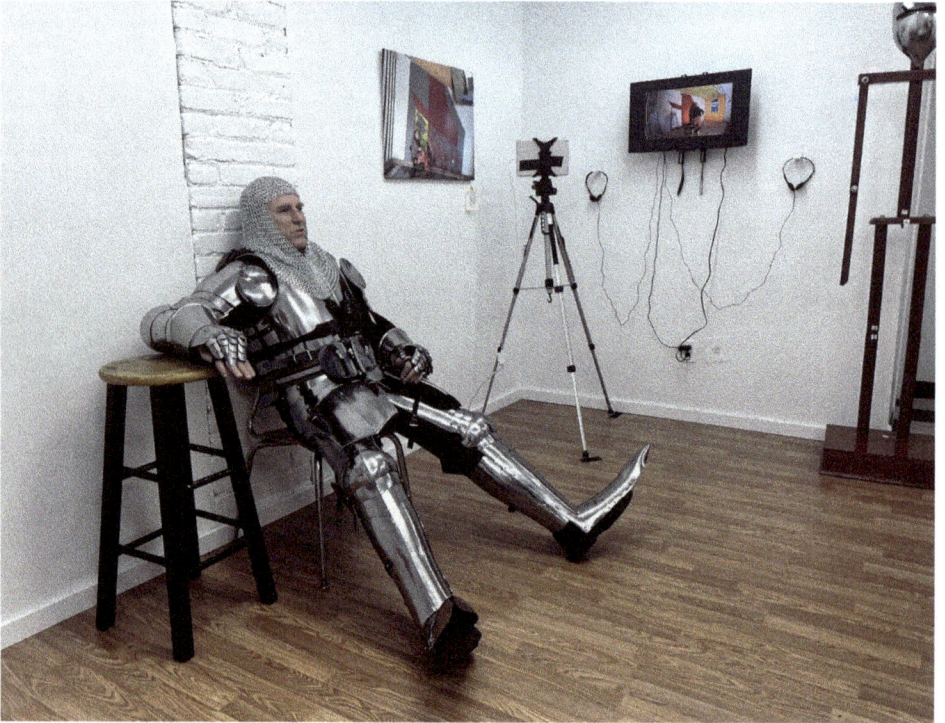

www.ingramcontent.com/pod-product-compliance
Lightning Source LLC
Chambersburg PA
CBHW060232030426
42335CB00014B/1421